**Rory**

# Saint George

Bloomsbury Methuen Drama
An imprint of Bloomsbury Publishing Plc

# B L O O M S B U R Y

LONDON · OXFORD · NEW YORK · NEW DELHI · SYDNEY

**Bloomsbury Methuen Drama**

An imprint of Bloomsbury Publishing Plc

Imprint previously known as Methuen Drama

| 50 Bedford Square | 1385 Broadway |
| London | New York |
| WC1B 3DP, UK | NY 10018, USA |

**www.bloomsbury.com**

**BLOOMSBURY, METHUEN DRAMA and the Diana logo
are trademarks of Bloomsbury Publishing Plc**

First published 2017

© Rory Mullarkey, 2017

Rory Mullarkey has asserted his right under the Copyright, Designs
and Patents Act, 1988, to be identified as author of this work.

**British Library Cataloguing-in-Publication Data**

A catalogue record for this book is available from the British Library.

ISBN: PB: 978-1-3500-6443-0
ePDF: 978-1-3500-6444-7
eBook: 978-1-3500-6445-4

**Library of Congress Cataloging-in-Publication Data**

A catalog record for this book is available from the Library of Congress.

Series: Modern Plays

Cover photography (John Heffernan) by David Stewart

Typeset by Country Setting, Kingsdown, Kent CT14 8ES
Printed and bound in Great Britain

To find out more about our authors and books visit www.bloomsbury.com.
Here you will find extracts, author interviews, details of forthcoming events
and the option to sign up for our newsletters.

## Acknowledgements

The process of making this text has been thoroughly iterative, which is a euphemistic way of saying I've done lots of drafts, and changed it frequently, and radically, since its very first version. This means the text could well be evolving even after its publication date, and so if you're interested in mounting a production of it (and, with 21+ actors and a flying dragon necessary, who wouldn't be?) then please contact my agents, Casarotto Ramsay and Associates, for an up-to-date version.

So many of the play's lines, ideas and theatrical gestures would not have materialised had it not been for a good number of workshops and readings. And so I'd like to thank Rufus Norris, Ben Power and everyone at the National Theatre, particularly in the New Work Department, who afforded ample opportunity for the play, and me, to breathe and to grow. I'd also like to thank all the actors, creatives, colleagues, agents, distinguished academics, friends and loved ones, who read the text and contributed thoughts at various stages of its genesis.

And I'd like to give particular thanks to Lyndsey Turner, who had the original idea for the play, and who ushered it into the world at every stage of its journey. Thank you, Lyndsey, for this and for so much more.

This piece began its life as a riff on Evgenii Schwartz's 1943–4 play *Drakon* (*The Dragon*). And though, in the intervening years of work, the text moved too far away from its source material to justify the continued use of the slippery label 'adaptation', the key dramatic conceit of the piece, along with a few of the character names (albeit anglicised), and a couple of exchanges in the first act, remain the same. And so I gratefully acknowledge the significant debt *Saint George and the Dragon* bears to Evgenii Schwartz, and to his brave and wonderful play.

Rory Mullarkey

# Saint George and the Dragon

*Saint George and the Dragon* received its world premiere on the Olivier stage of the National Theatre, London, on 11 October 2017. The cast, in alphabetical order, was as follows:

| | |
|---|---|
| **Fielder Sisters** | Suzanne Ahmet, |
| | Sharita Oomeer, |
| | Kirsty Rider |
| **Crier** | Jason Barnett |
| **Dragon** | Julian Bleach |
| **Young Miller** | Luke Brady |
| **Pike** | Paul Brennen |
| **Smith** | Joe Caffrey |
| **Mr Butcher** | Paul Cawley |
| **Henry** | Richard Goulding |
| **Charles** | Gawn Grainger |
| **Healer** | Tamzin Griffin |
| **Boy** | Reuel Guzman, |
| | Lewin Lloyd |
| **George** | John Heffernan |
| **Miller** | Stephanie Jacob |
| **Mrs Butcher** | Olwen May |
| **Driver** | Victoria Moseley |
| **Pike's Son** | Conor Neaves |
| **Elsa** | Amaka Okafor |
| **Brewer** | Jeff Rawle |
| **Healer's Daughter** | Grace Saif |

*Director*   Lyndsey Turner
*Designer*   Rae Smith
*Choreographer*   Lynne Page
*Lighting Designer*   Bruno Poet
*Music*   Grant Olding
*Sound Designer*   Christopher Shutt
*Fight Director*   Bret Young
*Company Dialect Work*   Majella Hurley
*Company Voice Work*   Rebecca Cuthbertson, Charmian Hoare
*Staff Director*   Guy Jones

## Characters

George
Charles
The Boy
Elsa
Henry
The Dragon
Brewer
Mr Butcher
Mrs Butcher
Crier
Pike
Pike's Son
Driver
Miller
Young Miller
Ann Fielder
Amy Fielder
Alice Fielder
Healer
Healer's Daughter
Smith
Guards
Voices
Homeless Man

## Act One: Village

### Chapter I
IN WHICH THE KNIGHT GEORGE ARRIVES HOME

### George

A knyght ther was, and that a worthy man,
That fro the tymé that he first bigan
To riden out, he lovéd libertie;
Thoughte all free-born, and all must liveth free.
A noble hearte, firm voice, visage ful-fair,
Bryght-twinkling eyes and sunryse-russette hair:
These fyne and fulsome qualities did merge
To forme this figure here, yclept Sir George.
When yonge, George join'd a Brotherhood of knyghts,
Who'd wonne bryght fame in many famous fyghts
'Gainst beasts both mythic and non-mythical:
Grendel and Sphynx, serpente and cannibal;
Unto this saintlie bande he pledg'd his hearte,
And studi'd ther to prove his knyghtlie arte.
He train'd his arms, his fingers and his calves,
And master'd maces, daggers, bludgeons, staves,
Untille, one daye, he heard a trumpet-sounde,
Which seem'd to pierce the aether all arounde
And meant that George had pass'd the Brothers' teste,
And so he would be granted his firste queste.
A dragon 'twas, that kepte its dreadfulle laire
Neare some smalle towne, and scourg'd the people there.
George took the offer'd armour, sword and shield,
And, swagg'ring, went to face it in the field.
Yet when he charg'd the beast it knock'd him downe,
Then sette about to massacre the towne.
George 'scap'd alone, alive: his scarréd breaste
The sole prize from this most ille-fat'd queste.
The Brothers call'd him back, to carry on;
They said 'Not ev'ry battle can be wonne':
George listen'd not. He lefte. He felte he'd fail'd:

Thus ended he his brief and knyghtlie tale.
He wander'd, then, thro' dulle dayes without number,
Untille, heartsicke, he felle into a slumber,
And in the warming bosom of a dreame
A vision of his home upon him came:
His home! The glist'ring isle where George was gat!
Wher all folk were unfetter'd: this isle sat
Safe and free and fair and sonnelyght-fill'd,
The land belong'd to all, rich fields were till'd
By all the folk, and swich a folk they were!
Fine-fac'd, true-tongu'd, inventive, brave and pure:
He sawe himself among them, there, contente:
Desire dissolv'd, his wreck'd ambition spente:
A little patch of lande, a little lyf!
A goat or two, perhaps! Perhaps a wyf!
He woke, resolv'd to seeke his native loam,
So built himself a barque and sailéd home.
But as George moor'd and slowly strode inlande
The change strucke him. He didn't understand:
The sonne, once ever-present, sat obscur'd
By thicke, grim cloudes, which black'd the air and lour'd
Their bulkes above the lande in the sicke sky;
The field-sodde, once fresh, rich, look'd charr'd and dry:
Was this the lande he lefte? Their houses, too:
Squatte hovels, hunch'd and crude, came into view;
George look'd up and the cloudes look'd ripe to burst,
His crack'd and barren throat was thicke with thirst,
So, glimpsing the next homestead's open door,
He wander'd thro and once inside he saw
An old man and a boy who flinch'd in fear
As if to say: 'What business have you here?'

**Charles**   What business have you here?

**George**   I'm neither a rogue nor a robber, sir: merely a
traveller, weary from the road.

**Charles**   Forgive me: where are my manners? Welcome, sir.
My name is Charles.

**George**   I'm George.

**Charles**   Pleased to meet you.

**George**   Might I trouble you, Charles, for a simple sip of water?

**Charles**   Of course (*Goes to fetch water.*) You've wandered far indeed, George, if you've strayed to this distant, lowly isle. Are you a stranger here?

**George**   Oh no, sir: I was born in this place.

**Charles** (*giving him the water*)   Well, in that case: welcome home.

**George**   I cannot tell you how much it cheers my heart, to come to a cottage and see a man and his son –

**Boy**   I'm not his son, I'm an orphan.

**George**   And see a man and his . . . resident orphan –

**Boy**   I'm not a resident, I live in the woods.

**George**   And see a man and his forest-dwelling orphan-boy –

**Boy**   It's not a forest –

**George**   It's good to be home, is all I meant. Although I find this place much changed.

**Charles**   How so?

**George**   Well, where is the sunlight that used to pour down on the land? Where is the birdsong that filled the bright air with its music?

**Charles**   Long gone, I'm afraid. These days are dark and silent.

**George**   Who rules here now?

**Charles**   Why, His Majesty the Dragon.

**George**   There's a dragon?

*He reels.*

**Charles**  Are you all right, sir?

**George** (*dazed*)  I flee a fight with one dragon only to be faced with another.

**Charles**  A fight with a dragon?! Are you, by some slim chance, a knight, sir?

**George**  I am. Well, I was.

**Boy**  He's a knight, Charles, he's a knight!

**George**  No, boy –

**Charles**  Oh, heavens!

**Boy**  He can save Elsa!

**George**  Who's Elsa?

**Charles**  My daughter.

**Boy**  The dragon's going to eat her tomorrow!

**George**  What?

**Boy**  He's going to tie her to a pole and eat her!

**Charles**  She's to be a sacrifice, George. Once a year the Dragon demands a maid be –

**Boy**  Burn her alive and eat her!

**Charles**  It's a kind of annual tradition, George –

**Boy** (*to* **George**)  But now you're here! (*To* **Charles**.) He's here, Charles!

**Charles**  Yes, now *you're* here: a knight of the Brotherhood, here, in my very own kitchen!

**George** (*realising where this is going*)  Oh, no –

**Charles**  It cannot be blind coincidence, George: the night before the feast and you arrive!

**George**  Apologies, but –

**Charles**  And so we're asking you, sir:

**Boy**   We're begging you, George.

**Charles** *and* **Boy**   Please save her!

**George**   I am sorry, but my answer is no. I have forsworn my former life, Charles, once and for all.

**Charles**   I know something of dragons, sir: I have dwelt beneath the hard fist of one for many a year now. I have tasted of its tyranny and trembled at its terror. But I know something of knights, too, sir, and the oath you swore can never be forsworn. You pledged yourself to protect those in danger: no knight ever born could sit by while the life of a fair maid lies at stake, oh no, sir: not while a heart still beats hot in his body!

**George** (*pulling down his tunic to show his scar*)   And what if that heart had been half near torn out by a beast of the very same breed? (*He starts to leave.*) I thank you kindly for the water, Charles, but there is not a maid in all the world who could ever turn my head towards that task, none, none, be she the fairest maid who ever lived!

**Elsa** *comes on.*

**Elsa** (*not noticing* **George**)   Good evening, Father, I know I'm late –

**Charles**   Daughter, I –

**Elsa**   So as if the indignity of being measured for the pole was not enough, Henry insisted that I practise being festooned with herbs to 'season' me for the sacrifice. I've been picking parsley out of my hair all the way home –

*She sees* **George**, *and stops. They stare at each other.*

**Charles**   George, this is Elsa, my daughter.

**George**   Meased to pleet you.

**Elsa**   I'm sorry?

**George**   Pleased to meet you.

**Elsa**    Who is this man, Father?

**Charles** (*moving* **George** *towards the door*)    He's nothing, Elsa, he's no one, a wanderer stopped in for some water, but he's leaving now.

**George** (*coming back into the room*)    Well perhaps not right away.

**Boy**    But you just said –

**George** (*going to* **Elsa**)    Maid, is it true you're to be devoured on the morrow?

**Elsa**    It is.

**George**    So no more will your eyes look upon the world?

**Elsa**    As grim a world as it is to look upon, I'll see it no more.

**George**    And no more will your fair cheek feel the morning sun?

**Elsa**    As dim a sun as it is to feel, I'll feel it no more.

**George**    And no more will your sweet breath brighten the sad air around you?

**Elsa**    If you can smell my breath from where you stand, sir, I do wonder that you think it sweet.

**George**    And no more will your ears –

**Elsa**    I'll spare you the trouble, sir: tomorrow ears, breath, cheek, eyes and all shall be scorched to cinders and devoured by the Dragon. And though it will be painful and prolonged, and though I shall be forced to wear a rather enormous hat made of herbs, which I find extremely undignified, I am resolved to bear it.

**George**    How big is this dragon?

**Charles**    The size of a barn.

**George**    I see. And how many legs does he have?

**Boy**    Four.

**George**    I understand. And how many claws?

**Boy**    Five on each foot.

**George**    Twenty in total. That's manageable. Any fangs?

**Charles**    Yes, indeed.

**Boy**    Sharp as knives.

**George**    Are they? Right.

**Charles**    And armoured all over with scales.

**Boy**    And big spikes on his tail!

**George**    Tail-spikes? As in spikes on the tail itself −

**Charles**    Not to mention the fire.

**George**    So he's a fire-breather? You didn't mention that.
Just the one head, though?

**Boy**    Three heads.

**George**    Because, yes, you see, three is rather a lot of −
(*Steeling himself.*) No, this maid is my countrywoman, and this
land is my home: however many heads he has, I care not!
I will challenge the Dragon!

**Boy**    Yes!

**Charles**    I knew it!

**Elsa**    What?!

**George**    Dragon, I challenge you!

**Elsa**    No!

*A shriek from the sky. A rumble in the air.* **Henry** *bursts into the
cottage, bearing a large horn.*

**Henry**    Kneel now, O pitiable subjects, and quake before
your sovereign: bringer of justice and fiery punishment,
master of all he surveys and possessor of all that surrounds
him; the sole and sceptred ruler of the island, His Majesty
the Dragon!

**Charles** *and the* **Boy** *kneel.*

**Henry**   You too, Elsa.

**Elsa** (*kneeling reluctantly*)   Yes, Henry.

**Henry**   Long live the Dragon!

**All**   Long live the Dragon!

**Henry** *blows the horn. A man dressed all in black enters the room.*

**Man**   Good evening to you all. The wind brought me word of a challenge.

**George** *is still looking at the door.*

**Man**   Stranger, why do you gaze goggle-eyed at the doorway?

**George**   Forgive me, sir, but this is rather an inopportune time for conversation. I'm expectant of the arrival of a dragon.

**Man**   You may expect no longer.

**George**   I beg your pardon?

**Man**   I am the Dragon.

**George**   You are the Dragon?

**Man**   I am the Dragon.

**George**   You are the three-headed, fire-breathing, barn-sized dragon?

**Man**   Yes.

**Henry**   His Majesty has lived so long among his subjects that he often makes his visits in his manly garb.

**Dragon**   I find it significantly easier for the entering of kitchens.

**George**   Ah.

**Dragon**   And thus: the challenge . . .

**George**   I am Sir George, knight of the Brotherhood, native to this isle, and for the life of the maiden you intend to devour,

and for the liberty of my dear countrymen, Dragon, I
challenge you!

*Silence.*

**Dragon**   Are you sure?

**George**   I'm sorry?

**Dragon**   Are you quite sure you wish to go through all that
again? I have a Brotherhood of my own, you see, Sir George,
and we speak across the winds to one another. The whisper
goes that the last time you tried to vanquish one of my kind it
didn't end well for you. And that you have the scar to prove it.
Could you hear them, while you walked away: the screams of
the men and the women and the children as he lined them all
up, and cooked them alive? Can you hear them, still, when
you close your eyes? Your fame has spread far and wide: Sir
George the Dragon-fleer. What makes you believe it will end
any differently this time?

**George**   This is the isle where I was born, and my fate
demands I scourge you from it. My challenge stands.

**Dragon**   Very well. I accept it. And as your opponent I will
set the terms. Henry, take them down.

**Henry** (*producing a scroll and a quill, and beginning to write*)   Yes,
Majesty. Thus: a fight to the death?

**Dragon**   To the death.

**Henry**   The time?

**Dragon**   At what hour do I devour the maid?

**Henry**   Half past midday.

**Dragon**   Then noon.

**Henry**   The place?

**Dragon**   The air above the village square.

**George**   In the sky?!

**Dragon**   Worry not, knight: I shall give you a loan of a carpet for the purpose

**Henry**   Very well. (*Writing.*) 'Flying carpet to be provided by His Majesty, along with the challenger's weapons.'

**George**   No, I will not take your weapons. I will ask the village to arm me.

**Henry**   But the custom dictates that –

**George**   I fight for my home and for my people. I'll wear no other armour save that which they bestow.

**Dragon**   But they are not your people, George. They're mine. I am sovereign of each hair upon their sorry subject heads. I am lord of the land they walk upon, possessor of each minute of their day. I am the strain of their waking hours and the terror of their sleep. I am the fist in their faces, the death of their friends, of their wives, of their dear daughters, and they would no more choose to arm you than they would challenge me themselves.

**George**   I know these people as I know myself. They'll recognise their own salvation when they see it.

**Dragon**   You *have* been away a long time, haven't you, George?

**George**   This is my only condition.

**Henry**   Majesty?

**Dragon**   I accept. The knight may petition the people for arms.

**Henry** (*writing*)   'Arms to be provided by the people.' (*Starting to roll up the scroll.*) The business is concluded, then.

**Dragon**   No, wait a moment, Henry. I might just add a condition of my own. If they are indeed foolish enough to take you as their champion, Sir George, they'd better hope you win: for if you lose I will destroy every one of them, man, woman and child, the whole island over.

**Henry**    But, Majesty, isn't that a little −

**Dragon**    These are my terms. (*To* **George**.) Shall Henry set them down?

**George**    Set them down.

**Dragon**    Very well. Tomorrow, then, sir.

**George**    Yes, tomorrow.

**Dragon**    Twelve o' the clock.

**George**    Excellent.

**Dragon**    Don't be late.

**George**    I shan't be.

**Dragon**    Have a pleasant evening.

**George**    You too.

**Dragon** (*raising his hat to her*)    Elsa.

*The* **Dragon** *swoops out, followed by* **Henry**.

**Elsa** (*to* **George**)    What on Earth have you done?!

**George**    I have pledged my life in defence of yours, Elsa, and I have done it gladly! Have you a keepsake about your person?

**Elsa**    A what?

**George** (*noticing her handkerchief*)    That handkerchief ought to do it, there, perfect.

**Elsa**    You're not taking my handkerchief.

**George** (*taking her handkerchief*)    I will bear this with me as I fight for your freedom.

**Elsa**    I didn't ask you to do this, George: nobody asked you to do this!

**Charles**    I did.

**Elsa**    Father!

**Boy**   And me!

**George**   Fear not, maid: when the people see I am come to save them, they will take me as their champion. And once I've defeated the monster, I will cut you free from that foul pole myself. (*To* **Charles**.) Now, Charles, have you somewhere I can lay my head? I ought to preserve my might for the morrow.

**Charles**   You may sleep by the fireside, sir.

**George**   Then good night to you all. Good night, sweet Elsa.

*He goes.*

**Boy** (*calling after him*)   Good night, George!

**Elsa**   Run along now, boy. It's time you were gone.

**Boy**   What? But what about the stew?

**Elsa**   Run along.

**Boy**   But I'm hungry!

**Elsa** (*sharply*)   Just go!

**Boy**   Fine. Good night.

*The* **Boy** *goes.*

**Charles**   Are you sure you don't want any of that stew?

**Elsa**   Did he tell you of his past, Father, when you begged him to fight for my life? Did he tell you he was no knight at all, but a coward?

**Charles**   No, he did not. Or perhaps he did, but –

**Elsa**   Then why did you allow him to –

**Charles**   Because I love you, my darling! I saw a chance to save your life and I took it. And I will not apologise for that. I will lay down to sleep this night with hope in my heart. The village may yet arm him, Elsa.

**Elsa**   That's precisely what I'm afraid of, Father. Good night.

**Charles** *goes. Silence. A knock at the door.* **Elsa** *turns, picks up a loaf of bread and goes to the door.*

**Elsa**    Fine, boy, you may take some bread, but then you must leave us in peace.

*She opens the door.* **Henry** *is there.*

**Henry**    Just a small slice for me, I mustn't stay.

**Elsa**    Henry –

**Henry**    Worry not, Elsa, I won't keep you long.

**Elsa**    This isn't going to be one of those times, is it, Henry, where you say you won't keep me long, then proceed to stand in my kitchen for hours on end? Because I'm really not in the humour –

**Henry**    I'm here about the knight.

**Elsa**    That was my father's doing, not mine: if it were up to me he'd never have returned to these wretched shores in the first place!

**Henry**    Which brings me briskly to my business here. I bear with me an offer from His Majesty.

**Elsa**    An offer?

**Henry** (*taking out a scroll and reading it*)  'His Majesty the Dragon does hereby pledge, that if Elsa the maid does him the gentle kindness of slitting Sir George's throat this night as he sleeps –'

**Elsa**    Slit his throat?! I won't take a life, Henry.

**Henry**    Not even in exchange for your own?

**Elsa**    I beg your pardon?

**Henry**    Listen: 'He will forgo his annual feast on the morrow, and spare the life of the maid.'

*Silence.*

(*Producing a dagger.*) He offers you his very own dagger for the purpose.

*Silence.*

**Elsa**   I won't do it, Henry.

**Henry**   But your life –

**Elsa**   I don't care about my life.

**Henry**   Then do it for the village. They'll never vote to arm the knight, you know that. But they'll tear themselves to pieces in the process. And if, by some strange miracle, they do, then in return the Dragon will pour his fiery hell on all of us!

**Elsa**   Well, not on you, Henry.

**Henry**   Elsa, please, I know that you hold no affection for me, and I understand that, I do, but it is not I who threatens the safety of the people here, nor His Majesty neither. The threat is the arrogant fool asleep by your fireside there, so if you have any sense in you at all, you'll get rid of him tonight, remove the threat, for the sake of every person on this island.

*Silence.* **Elsa** *takes the dagger.*

**Elsa**   It's the right thing to do. Long live the Dragon.

*He goes.* **Elsa** *stands, alone, and examines the dagger.*

### Chapter II
IN WHICH GEORGE FACES THE DRAGON

*The village square, the following morning. The villagers gather for the meeting, household by household, chattering anxiously as they go.* **Charles** *is there, but* **Elsa** *is not.* **Crier** *rings his bell, as* **Brewer**, *at the centre, stands.*

**Crier**   Silence, I pray you, for the village meeting. Silence!

*Silence quickly descends.*

**Brewer**    I thank you. Now. You know wherefore we've all been called together. And being, as I am, your village inn-keep, and hence a man well-practised in the art of mediation, I have been chosen to lead this meeting; though the matter that sits before us today is far more grave than any drink dispute could ever hope to be. I know that not everyone in the village is present: either the weight of their work forbids them, or their fear of the matter prevents them, but those of you who speak for them today, may you stand and declare yourselves now.

**Pike**    Pike, village guard.

**Son**    Pike, his son.

**Miller**    Miller and her son. Village millers.

**Crier** (*extremely loud*)    Crier, village crier.

**Driver**    Driver, driver of oxen.

**Mrs Butcher**    Butcher, village butcher.

**Mr Butcher**    Butcher – (*Simultaneously with* **Mrs Butcher**.) Her husband.

**Mrs Butcher** (*simultaneously*)    My husband.

**Ann Fielder**    Fielder; and my two sisters. Land workers.

**Healer**    Healer, village healer.

**Healer's Daughter**    Healer, her daughter.

**Brewer** (*to* **Charles**, *who is looking off*)    And you, Charles.

**Charles**    What? Oh, yes.

**Brewer**    Will your daughter be joining us too?

**Charles**    I know not where she is: she wasn't there to be woken this morning, and her bed looked unslept-in all night –

**Mrs Butcher**    I wouldn't worry yourself, Charles, she'll not have gone far.

**Charles**    You're right, Butcher. Of course.

**Brewer** Very well: to business, then. (*Calling out.*) Let the knight approach!

**George** *arrives in the square, and walks to the centre.*

**Alice Fielder** Is that him?!

**Ann Fielder** Shhh!

**Alice Fielder** He's a knight?!

**Ann Fielder** Quiet, Alice!

**Alice Fielder** He don't look much like a knight.

**Brewer** (*to* **George**) Sir, you may have your brief say.

**George** Good morrow to you all. I am Sir George, knight of the Brotherhood, native to this isle. I have returned to this place to vanquish the Dragon and win you your freedom. So if you'd kindly oblige me with arms –

**Driver** Oblige you, sir?

**George** Yes, oblige me with arms.

**Driver** Look, I care not who you are –

**George** Sir George, I believe I made that clear –

**Driver** Our very lives sit in the balance here. So if we're to grant this petition of yours we'll need more to go on than the hopes of a man we know not at all!

**Charles** He is a knight, madam! That is all you need to know. He has challenged the Dragon according to the code of his Brotherhood, and is willing to place his blood and body on the line to slay him and to rescue my daughter!

**Miller** I understand you, Charles. You are Elsa's father. She is your daughter. You want to save her. You love her. I see. But though this village be not big, there are more in it than simply you and she.

**Brewer**   She's right, Charles: this matter is a wide one, indeed. And I know that our tempers run hot around the Dragon's feast day –

**Mrs Butcher**   Our tempers run hot the whole year long, Brewer! Yes, today is the Dragon's feast day, but what was it you said about it, husband, do you remember, you were gibleting a pheasant at the time, do you remember what you said about it?

**Mr Butcher**   I said every day is his –

**Mrs Butcher**   He said, 'Every day is his feast day.' Every day is his feast day, sirs, and it's true, is it not? My husband and I are the butchers here, it's our work to slaughter the village livestock and cut them up into chops, or chop them up into cuts, depending, of course: pork, mutton, poultry, game, all of it, and then we –

**Mr Butcher**   Beef.

**Mrs Butcher**   Beef, too, precisely, yes, and then we take it over to the Dragon's cave: huge great hillocks of meat, the cart groaning under the heft of it. And what little is left, what pitiable scraps remain after he's gorged himself –

**Mr Butcher**   Tripe, mostly.

**Mrs Butcher**   Mostly tripe, indeed – we're permitted to give to the rest of the village. And it's not just our meat that he filches but our ale, and our flour –

**Mr Butcher**   And our wheat.

**Mrs Butcher**   Precisely, and our corn and our barley, too. And our children. Tell him, Healer.

*Everyone looks at* **Healer**.

**Mrs Butcher**   Tell him.

**Healer**   I can't.

**Mrs Butcher**   The knight needs to know.

**Healer**   Very well. I'm the healer of the village, knight. And fate bestowed upon me two beautiful daughters. The Dragon devoured the eldest one shortly before her eighteenth birthday. She met her end, right there – (*Points.*) with all of us watching. The light went out of the world, that day. I'll never . . .

**Mrs Butcher** (*tender*)   It's all right, dear. Keep going.

**Healer**   My youngest is a few weeks shy of her seventeenth year. A girl born even more fair than the first. And I love her as she is, of course: she is my very own, but I prayed on the morning she came kicking out of me that she be a boy and my heart dropped when I saw that she wasn't. And folk come to me with their wounds and their ailments, and I heal them as best I can. Yet the person I love the most on this Earth is stricken with a terror I can't cure. Nights I've found her hacking at her hair with a carving knife, I . . . I . . .

**Mrs Butcher**   And tell him what she said when you found her.

**Healer** *shakes her head.*

**Mrs Butcher**   What did she say, Healer?

**Brewer**   Now, Butcher –

**Healer's Daughter**   I said I don't want to be pretty.

**Mrs Butcher**   You see: it is a vile and criminal beast! He needs to be put from the world!

**Alice Fielder**   Oh, I'd smash him myself if I could: bash his face with our father's shovel!

**Ann Fielder**   Alice, what have I told you about talking? I said when I brung you here –

**Alice Fielder**   You know I'd do it, Ann! You just let me near him!

**Ann Fielder**   Alice, please.

**Alice Fielder**   Let me speak!

**Brewer**  Might we calm ourselves, you two? I know the mood is up –

**Amy Fielder**  Forgive my sisters, sir, but this subject was near indeed to our parents' dear hearts, before they were took from us. Our mother used to tell stories of the time before the Dragon, of days filled with light, and I, for one, would love to go back to that time!

**Crier** (*loud*)  I heard the self-same stories, sirs! The time before the Dragon! Forgive me, knight, but I am the crier of this village, and I feel I must speak up at this moment!

**George**  Yes, why not? Everyone else has had a go.

**Crier**  Whenever that lackey of his puts some new proclamation into my hand my heart shudders and sinks with the dark weight of it! I know I'll have to stand here in this square and cry something horrid: some vicious new tax, some barbaric new law, some sick and savage punishment for a crime that's no crime at all!

**Alice**  Too right!

**Crier**  And then I think of all the stories my father used to tell, of the time before the Dragon: of the square warm and sunny and brimming with life, of all the bright and happy news he used to cry: babies born and named, big weddings, revels to mark the bringing in of huge harvests, so if we could vanquish the Dragon and have that again –

**Driver**  Yes, we've all heard the stories, Crier, we've all dreamed him gone: d'you think I haven't slain him a thousand times myself, in my head? When I'm out on the land, shoving the plough through the earth, I dream I'm latticing up his ugly body: I think of that oftentimes and long. But whether or not we want that beast dead is not at issue today. We're all met to answer a question, and the question is this: can we take this man here as our champion?

**George**  I have the measure of this dragon, madam: he has three heads, four legs, twenty claws –

**Pike**   I'm sorry, sir, but you do not: that's not the measure of this monster. My son and I, we guard the Dragon's cave, don't we, son?

**Son**   Yes, Father.

**Pike**   It's our work to keep watch outside it, each day, as he scourges our friends and our neighbours. We're stood there, looking out, forbidden to move, dawn to dusk. So we've got knowledge of him more than most, haven't we, son?

**Son**   Yes, Father.

**Pike**   And I am a big man, sirs. I can just about take it. But I fear for my boy. He was born too small. Too good. We don't see the dreadful happenings of that place.

**Son**   There are sounds, though, Father.

**Pike**   There are, son. And smells.

**Son**   And feelings.

**Pike**   So heed me when I say to you, sir: whatever it is he's doing to them in there, he isn't doing with heads or legs or claws.

**Son**   All that we know is there's no one ever gone in who's ever come out.

**Miller**   There's one. My son, Sir George. He wandered in when he was little. What happened in that place –

**Young Miller**   The, the, the, the, the –

**Miller**   Peace now, boy. The Dragon did not kill him when he caught him. He did something worse. He burned him, deep. He reached his flame right through my son's skin and into his soul, and he seared himself there. You see him now. The Dragon did this. To a child. There is a word for it. Evil. Do you have the measure of that, sir? I'm not sure you do.

**George**   Of course, madam, I understand that –

**Driver**  If I may ask you, sir: how many dragons have you faced in the past?

**Charles**  Now, Driver, that hardly has bearing –

**Miller**  Answer the question, knight.

**Pike**  How many?

**George**  Around one.

**Driver**  And how many have you killed?

**Charles**  That really does not –

**Brewer**  Charles –

**Driver**  The village deserves an answer, knight.

*Silence.*

**George**  None.

**Driver**  Then we're done here: the matter is plain.

**George**  But, madam, that really does not affect –

**Son**  We arm him, we die. Is that it, Father?

**Pike**  Yes, son. Most likely.

**George**  Sir, you underestimate me.

**Crier**  Well now you say that, it seems better not to arm him at all.

**George**  Better for whom? Better for the Dragon, perhaps! Better –

**Brewer**  Knight, we thank you kindly. But the mood among us here is strong. Let us put it to a vote.

**Elsa** *runs on.*

**Charles**  Daughter!

**George**  Elsa!

**Charles**  Where have you been?!

**Elsa** (*panting*)  Listen to me, please, before you . . . Henry came to our cottage late last night, and he bore with him a proposition from His Majesty: that if I slew the knight while he slept, I myself would 'scape the painful death that is ordained for me this day. He gave me this dagger for that purpose.

*She shows the village the dagger.*

**Pike**  That's the Dragon's dagger, isn't it, son?

**Son**  Yes, Father. He never ventures anywhere without it.

**Driver**  Why's the knight still here, then? Why took you not his offer?

**Elsa**  I couldn't do it. Something stopped me. I thought it was compassion. It wasn't that. Weakness, perhaps? But no, it was something else, something that nagged and gnawed at my brain, something that didn't make sense: if His Majesty is truly almighty, why would he wish me to murder the knight? And then it hit me: the Dragon must be scared.

**Driver**  Scared?

**Elsa**  I've got you wrong, Sir George: the Dragon must be terrified of you.

**George**  No, you've got me exactly right, Elsa. The last and only time I fought a dragon, sirs, I failed. And this – (*Shows his scar.*) was my reward. He isn't scared of me. He's scared of you.

**Miller**  Scared of us?

**George**  I confess that I came here today thinking you'd grant my petition in a heartbeat, that you'd swoon in wonder at the very sight of me: the mighty knight returned!

**Charles**  We meant no offence, sir –

**George**  No, Charles, the fault was all mine. I've been so long away that I'd forgot you. You are the folk who first fixed three wheels to a little box, so that you might bear more than what your tired arms could carry; you are the folk who first employed the wax of bees to light your homes, so you might tell your children tales as they lie abed at night; who ground little circles of glass so a sightless man could see; who first combined the twin joys of apples and pastry! And though this place is small, and though it's rainy, and though you do not shy from complaint, and enjoy standing often in line for little reason: you are yet mighty. You are not a people to live hunched and cowed, beneath a tyrant's yoke: no, not you. Not us. Of course the Dragon's scared. He's scared that we might dare to dream a world without his rule. But isn't that a dream worth risking everything for? We may yet lose our lives today, my friends, but to die boldly, full-blood, for the better, in the grip of some great idea: there is far more life in that kind of death; and far, far more death in the other kind of life!

**Alice Fielder**   Yes!

**Mrs Butcher**   Well said, sir!

**Healer**   We stand with you, knight!

**Crier**   We're with you, sir!

**Driver**   So what shall we arm him with, then?

*Silence.*

**Miller**   We've got nothing, just the mean tools of our trades.

**Brewer**   Odds and ends.

**Amy Fielder**   Bits and bobs.

**Crier**   Pots and . . . you know, the flat pots.

**Smith** *arrives, wheeling something large and covered.*

**Smith**   Apologies, apologies, some final tweaks were necessary, apologies – (*He sees* **George**.) Are you the – Oh, goodness it's truly you, isn't it? This is truly happening, isn't it?

**Brewer**   Smith: what is the meaning of this?

**Smith**   Oh, goodness, I hope I be not late, am I late? My wife, you see, she's rather stern, lovely woman, but she did,

I suppose, forbid me to be here, but I'm here, I suppose, and so: yes. The thing is: I knew you'd come one day, well, not you exactly, but a hero, someone to save us. My wife said it was all silliness, of course, she's rather stern, you see, but I believed it still, so I sought to be, I suppose, prepared. I'm the smith here, you see, and it's not an easy life, but I saved up any spare metal I could find, scraps, primarily, offcuts, you know, and I spent my evenings and early mornings, in secret, for the last, possibly, fifteen years, so when that day did come we might, perhaps, be ready.

*He unveils a gleaming suit of armour and a sword.*

So yes, it's a suit of armour, as you can see, with full-plate coverage, slatted for extra manoeuvrability and reinforced for strength against the hottest of fires, and there's a sword too, which is extremely sharp and should cut through anything, it's rather my life's work, you see. So I suppose the question is . . . will you wear it?

**George** (*humble*)   If . . . if you'll have me? Mr Brewer?

**Brewer**   Let us move to a vote, then. All those in favour of arming Sir George, say aye.

**All**   Aye!

**Brewer**   The motion is passed!

*A shriek from the air. A rumble in the sky.* **Henry** *bursts on.*

**Henry**   Bow your heads, O meek and servile vassals, and tremble before your monarch: liege of every corner of the land, and lord of all life that dwells upon it; the sole and sceptred ruler of the island, His Majesty the Dragon! Long live the Dragon!

*Silence.*

Has there been a sudden plague of deafness? Long live the Dragon!

*The* **Dragon** *walks into the square.*

**Dragon**    It's all right, Henry: we may dispense with the formalities on this occasion. Who here has charge of this gathering?

**Brewer**    I do.

**Dragon**    And has the village reached a decision?

**Brewer**    It has.

**Dragon**    Well?

**Brewer**    We hereby elect, by vote unanimous, to take Sir George as our champion, and do grant his petition for arms, that he may fight you, Dragon, this day, for the life of the maiden, and the liberty of us, the people of this isle!

**Dragon**    Very well.

*Silence. The* **Dragon** *slowly approaches the suit of armour.*

So these are the arms he'll be using, then, are they? Such dazzling craftsmanship. Your work, I presume, Smith?

**Smith**    Indeed.

**Dragon**    It must've taken a lifetime.

*The* **Dragon** *removes the left armpiece.*

Well. Villagers, I am . . . surprised. I never thought you'd pick this course of action. I thought my incentive against it was firm enough indeed. But no. I see. It's gone the other way. And now I must allow the knight to wear this . . . beautiful armour. Such were the terms of the challenge, I know, and an honourable man would abide by them. Yet I am not an honourable man: I AM A DRAGON!

*He breaks the armpiece in two and throws it to the floor.*

So first the maid breaks faith with me –

*He breaks the left legpiece in half.*

Then all of you choose to strike at my power: well I won't let that happen!

*He punches through the breastplate.*

You verminous, pitiable little wretches: I am your ruler!

*He tears apart the breastplate and the whole right side of the suit.*

And all of you must answer for your treason here today.

*He picks up the helmet and uses it like a puppet, speaking with the visor.*

'We hereby elect, by vote unanimous, to take Sir George as our champion!'

*He punches through the helmet.*

Death to your champion!

*He picks up the sword.*

And as for you, knight: you ought to know better.

*He snaps the sword in half.*

I am a foul and devilish reptile: I do not play fair!

**Henry** (*pulling out the contract*)   But, Majesty, the terms of the contract –

*The* **Dragon** *burns the contract to a crisp in* **Henry**'s *hands.*

**Dragon**   No more contracts! The time for terms is done! I will slay the knight, devour the maid, then destroy all the rest of you, once and for all! Now, haven't you all got a feast to prepare for?! Go!

*The villagers and* **Henry**, *terrified and crestfallen, rush out.* **George** *and the* **Dragon** *are alone.*

**George**   Dragon, this matter concerns you and me, alone: please don't slaughter the villagers, I beg you, sir.

**Dragon**   Slaughter them? Whatever gave you that idea, George?

**George**   You said you were going to destroy them.

**Dragon**   But I won't do that by killing them, George. Any fool can take a life. But where's the victory in that? I want to break them apart from within. I want to crush all that is good in them. I want to rip out their joy and their kindness. Until all that is left is mine. Until they become me. And you've helped me to do just that.

**George**   To help you?

**Dragon**   You gave them hope, Sir George. You made them believe this battle can be won. And when you die today, and you will die today, be assured of it, that hope will shatter into a thousand pieces, they'll know that this story will never end in their triumph, and they'll stare into the sunless future stretched out before them, and see, in the darkness, there, my smiling face. I'll see you in the sky.

*The* **Dragon** *strolls out.* **George** *slumps, despondent. The* **Boy** *approaches, holding several pots and pans, strung together with belts.*

**George**   What is it, boy?

**Boy**   I heard you at the meeting, George. I was hiding. I like what you said: 'A dream worth risking everything for!' It has a ring to it. I like it. (*Indicating the pots and pans.*) I've strung these together: they're for you.

**George**   I appreciate the gesture, boy. But I'll have no need of cooking apparatus where I'm going.

**Boy**   It's not just these, we've all brought something.

**Miller** *and* **Young Miller** *arrive, with a pipe.*

**Miller**   Our grain scoop.

**Brewer** *arrives, bearing a grate.*

**Brewer**   A metal grate.

**Healer** *and* **Daughter** *arrive, with a length of rope.*

**Healer's Daughter**   A length of rope.

*The* **Fielder Sisters** *arrive, with a boot-scraper.*

**Ann Fielder**   A boot-scraper.

**Mrs Butcher** *and* **Mr Butcher** *arrive, with plates.*

**Mrs Butcher**   Our best plates.

**Driver** *arrives, with a mallet.*

**Driver**   A wooden mallet.

**Smith** *arrives, with a rusty sword.*

**Smith**   A rusty sword.

**Charles** *arrives, with a bolt of cloth.*

**Charles**   A roll of cloth.

**Crier** *arrives, with a little colander.*

**Crier**   A . . . You know, you put food in there and the water comes out. You know, for the food.

*The villagers stand, holding their objects.*

**George**   Good folk, these gifts –

**Boy**   They're not gifts, George. We thought it might serve as your armour.

*They display their objects, to form a makeshift suit of armour.*

**George**   But I can't take this, I –

*The folk begin to bundle up the armour for* **George**. *Meanwhile* **Elsa** *has arrived, bound and garlanded, followed by* **Pike** *and* **Son**, *who are carrying a large pole.* **Pike** *and* **Son** *begin to erect the pole.* **Elsa** *goes to* **George**.

**Elsa**   We know what we're doing, George. We know you might die. And we know what will happen if you do.

**George**   Then why are you doing this?

**Elsa**   Because we've decided to believe. And if the Dragon won't honour his contract, then we'll at least honour ours. (*Pulling out the* **Dragon**'s *dagger.*) Here: take this knife.

**George**   The Dragon's dagger?

**Elsa**    He never took it back. And you may have need of it, up there.

**George** (*taking the dagger*)    Did you really almost kill me with this in my sleep?

**Elsa**    George, I've known since my childhood I'd meet my end tied to that pole. I remember the moment so clearly. I was out in the field working, that field, just there, and I thought I was all on my own, and then I looked up, and Dragon was standing, stock still, at the edge, and he was watching. And he raised his hat to me. And I just knew. And something changed in that second, inside me, something closed and locked itself shut, and I spent every moment since grieving for the life I'd never have, for the sun I'd never see, for the future that would never be mine. But then –

**Henry** (*arriving, looking up*)    Form up, villagers, His Majesty is restless to commence!

**George**    Then what?

**Elsa**    Then this. Then now. Then you.

**George**    I –

**Henry** (*pushing **George** aside*)    No more speeches, man. (*To **Pike** and **Son**.*) Come on, secure her. (*Seeing the bundle of arms.*) And what's all this?

**George**    This is my armour, sir. And I am proud to wear it.

**Henry** (*laughing*)    Worthless armour for a worthless knight: how apt! Very well. (*Giving the bundle to **George**.*) Take it, then.

**George** *starts to go. The villagers form up into a line, ready to watch the fight.*

**Henry** (*parodying a herald, as **George** goes*)    Avert your eyes, O meek and woeful folk, and shudder for your champion: clutching his rusty sword and his collection of scraps, the pitiable harvester of the fruits of your sedition, the bringer of your imminent doom, Sir George the Dragon-fleer!

**Brewer**   I'm glad you're enjoying yourself, Henry.

**Henry**   Oh I am. (*Back to being a herald.*) Cower as he mounts his tattered, scrappy rug and heads to the sky! Oh, and marvel as His Majesty, resplendent in his full three-headed form, takes his position!

**Pike**   George doesn't look too clever on that carpet there, does he, son?

**Son**   No, Father.

**Henry**   Let battle commence!

*He blows his horn. The villagers stand in silence, watching the sky.*

Watch him, villagers: watch your ruler, screaming through the sky! Chasing that feeble knight through the air, then parting his jaws for a huge streak of flame! Yes, that's it, Your Majesty! Swipe him with your claws! Swat him from the air like a wayward fly –

*The villagers wince.*

Yes: got him! The knight's sped underneath you now, Your Majesty! But watch, O villagers, see the Dragon somersault over him, oh how graceful, then marvel as he dives down low to pluck him from the air!

*The villagers duck.*

The knight's darted on away: swoop back for another pass, Your Majesty!

*The villagers duck again.*

Yes, that's it: you're gaining on him now, you've got him in your sights, that's it, there's nowhere for the knight to run, that's it, that's it, you're catching up to him, your eyes are locked in the air, that's it, and you open your vast and dripping jaws to swallow him and –

*The villagers gasp.* **Henry***'s face falls. One of the* **Dragon***'s heads falls into the square with a crash.*

**Henry** (*taking out a scroll and reading it*)    Proclamation, urgent proclamation from His Majesty: the loss of one of his heads will only make him fly more swiftly through the sky! He is at the very cusp of defeating the challenger!

**Smith**    I knew all would be well as long as he had my blade!

*The sword falls out of the sky and clatters into the square.*

Ah.

**Henry**    Yes!

**Mrs Butcher**    The Dragon bashed it clean out of his hand with his tail!

**Pike**    Well, what will he do now, son?

**Son**    I don't know, Father.

**Driver**    He's done for: he's got no weapons.

**Henry**    And the Dragon's zooming back towards him to hit him again.

*The villagers duck.*

**Crier**    Be careful, George!

**Amy Fielder**    Not even a sword.

**Driver**    Be careful!

**Henry**    Oh watch as he scores him again with his talons!

*The villagers wince.*

**Healer**    Watch out now, George!

**Brewer**    He's looming over you!

**Henry**    He has no hope, Your Majesty! Nothing to use against you!

**Mrs Butcher**    I'm just praying he keeps on that carpet.

**Henry**    Rusted scraps, that's all he's got, Your Majesty!

**Brewer**    The Dragon's circling him now.

**Smith**   Oh poor man, he's done for!

**Henry**   He's helpless, Majesty, close in for the kill!

**Boy**   Look, George has darted away from him!

**Henry**   He's darted away but you can catch him, Majesty!

**Alice Fielder**   And he's taking the shovel off its handle and he's dodging the Dragon's blows!

**Smith**   That shovel blade's not sharp enough, girl!

**Ann Fielder**   No, he's not going to strike him with it –

**Boy**   He's rubbing it, polishing it with his sleeve!

**Henry**   You're close enough, Your Majesty: use your fire! Use your fire!

**Boy**   And look: he's holding up the shovel like a shield!

**Henry**   Flame him!

**Boy**   No, not like a shield: like a mirror!

*A blazing, scorching sound. The villagers gasp. The second **Dragon**'s head, charred and smoking, falls into the square with a crash.*

**Henry** (*taking out a scroll and reading it*)   Proclamation, urgent proclamation from His Majesty: he has at last attained his true, single-headed nature, the most fearsome of all his forms, and is at the very brink of destroying the knight –

**Elsa**   Oh shut up, Henry.

**Brewer**   Look at George go!

**Crier**   Go on, George!

**Healer**   Look at the knight up there!

**Healer's Daughter**   Look at him loop and spin in the air!

**Brewer**   Look at him go!

**Charles**   Such finesse!

**Smith**   Such aplomb!

**Miller**    Such control!

**Driver**    Look at him duck!

**Crier**    And weave and roll!

**Mr Butcher**    Yes –

**Mrs Butcher**    Look at him go!

*The sky darkens suddenly.*

**Boy**    But what's that?

**Healer**    What's that?

**Pike**    What's happening, son?

**Son**    Something's happening, Father.

**Elsa**    It's the Dragon.

**Miller**    The Dragon!

**Crier**    He's starting to grow!

**Ann Fielder**    He's growing.

**Brewer**    And growing.

**Young Miller**    The, the, the, the –

**Amy Fielder**    And growing.

**Healer's Daughter**    And growing.

**Driver**    He's massive!

**Smith**    The size of a mountain!

**Charles**    The size of a mountain!

**Boy**    He's angry.

**Elsa**    He's fuming.

**Alice Fielder**    The size of a mountain!

**Healer**    He'll make the knight pay.

**Mrs Butcher**    He turns and whips his tail!

**Mr Butcher**   No –

**Mrs Butcher**   Then swoops down and in for the kill!

**Boy**   Duck!

*The villagers duck as the carpet and* **George***'s other items fall from the sky. Silence.*

**Brewer**   Where is he?

**Crier**   Where's George gone?

**Pike**   Is that it? Is it over, son?

**Son**   I don't know, Father.

**Elsa**   No, because there he is hanging from the end of his tail!

**Boy**   Hanging from the rope!

**Healer**   And he hauls himself up the long length of rope.

**Smith**   And on to the Dragon himself.

**Driver**   And he locks his hands round the sharp spines that jut from its back.

**Healer's Daughter**   And he climbs the spines like stairs.

**Crier**   He's climbing.

**Brewer**   Up and up and up.

**Ann Fielder**   He's climbing.

**Charles**   But his feet trip and slip on the blood that runs down its back.

**Driver**   And the Dragon is thrashing and crashing about in mid-air.

**Mrs Butcher**   I can't watch!

**Mr Butcher**   But George holds on!

**Pike**   He holds on, doesn't he, son?

**Son**    He holds on.

**Smith**    And there's fire flaming from the nostrils now.

**Brewer**    And jets screaming out of the jaws.

**Miller**    But he holds on.

**Boy**    Hold on, George!

**Elsa**    Hold on.

**Crier**    And the Dragon is thrashing and crashing and crashing and thrashing.

**Amy Fielder**    And they're rolling about in mid-air.

**Charles**    But he's there!

**Elsa**    There at the edge of the neck and he pulls the Dragon's own dagger from his boot and plunges it with all his strength into the base of the skull and –

*Gasps. The **Dragon**'s body explodes in the air above. A shower of green and gold light. Silence.*

**Driver**    Is it over?

**Crier**    Is he . . . dead?

**Healer's Daughter**    Where's George?

**Boy** (*seeing* **George** *returning*)    There he is!

*A bird cries softly and breaks into song.*

**Miller**    And is that . . .

*More birds join the birdsong.*

**Charles**    The birds! They're back!

**Son**    Look: the mist's rising, Father!

**Pike**    I know, son.

**Amy Fielder**    The clouds are drifting away.

**Healer's Daughter**    And what's that?

**George** *arrives, wearing the makeshift armour and covered in blood.*

**Elsa** (*looking at* **George**)   The sun.

*The villagers cheer.* **Pike** *frees* **Elsa**. **Pike**'s **Son** *and* **Healer's Daughter** *spontaneously embrace, but then break away, shy and surprised. Everyone rushes over to congratulate* **George**.

**Charles**   You saved us, George! You won!

**Boy**   You're bleeding, George!

**Healer** (*bustling into action*)   Let's get that off you, sir. You're covered in blood.

**George**   What? It's mostly the Dragon's, I think.

**Alice Fielder**   You bashed him up good and proper, sir! That's what I like to see.

**Healer** *and* **Daughter** *help to remove* **George**'s *armour.*

**Mrs Butcher**   I couldn't watch you there for a moment, George, I just couldn't watch.

**George** (*to* **Healer's Daughter**)   I'm sorry I lost your rope.

**Healer's Daughter**   It doesn't matter.

**George** *stands, shorn of his armour. A large, bloody cross emblazons his tunic: a red cross on a white background.*

**Smith**   Would you look at that!

**Charles**   That's a true knightly sigil if ever I saw one, George.

**Elsa** (*who has finally got through the crowd*)   George!

**George** (*holding out her handkerchief*)   Your handkerchief, Elsa. I'm sorry. It wasn't mine to take.

**Elsa**   But it's yours now, George. For good. So keep it safe.

*They look at each other.*

You did it.

**George**   Well, it isn't done yet. We've won our liberty, but the land isn't ours until all that monster thieved from us is back in our hands.

**Henry**   We could start by destroying the cave.

**George** (*turning on* **Henry**)   I beg your pardon?

**Henry**   Well, there's plenty of treasure in the cave, is all I mean, so we could use that to –

**Crier**   Apologies, sir: who's 'we'?

**Henry**   Well, all of us. We're free now, George, and –

**Driver**   We are free, Henry. You are not.

**Pike**   You latched yourself on to that tyrant for years: what makes you think we won't grant you the same fate as him?

**Alice**   String the lackey up!

**George**   No, we shan't kill him. That may have been the Dragon's solution but it mustn't be ours. Pike.

**Pike**   Yes, George.

**George**   Lock him away in a windowless cell. The meanest, darkest place you can find. No: give him one window, so he may watch as we bring this isle into a golden age: as we build, invent, grow, trade and make this nation the envy of the world!

**Smith**   Let's get to work, then!

**George** (*taking* **Elsa**'*s hand*)   We've seen what we can achieve with a dragon, let's see what we can achieve without one!

**George** *and* **Elsa** *move to kiss, but a bright, high, piercing trumpet sounds.*

**Boy**   The Brotherhood!

**Charles**   It seems you have been summoned, George.

**George**   Summoned?

**Charles**   Well, you're Sir George the Dragon-slayer now, and though the sun smiles down on us once more, there are other lands, all across the Earth, still shrouded in shadow.

**George** *looks at* **Elsa**.

**George**   I –

**Elsa**   Go now, brave Sir George, and show the world what freedom looks like, and when you have finished, come back here, to me, come home, and I will be waiting for you, I promise.

**George** *smiles.*

**Elsa**   Will you do it quickly, though, please? I'd quite like my future to begin.

**George** *releases* **Elsa***'s hand, then starts to go. He stops.*

**George**   Wait: take this.

*He takes off his tunic.*

Bear this part of me with all of you, as I will bear a part of you with me, and sing your fame through all the world. Raise it as a banner: let this be the flag that guides me home.

*He gives the tunic to* **Elsa***, and goes.*

**Crier** *(ringing his bell)*   Oyez, oyez, oyez, the dreadful Dragon is dead! The sun smiles down on the land again! Today our freedom is won! Freedom from tyranny! Freedom for all, for all time!

## Act Two: Town

### Chapter III
#### IN WHICH SAINT GEORGE RETURNS

*A year passes, and the village becomes a town in front of us. The townsfolk achieve this themselves, it is done through the work of their hands and the sweat of their brows. It is an Industrial Revolution, and they are in the middle of it.*

*As they work, and setting and costume evolve, the townsfolk sing:*

**All** (*singing*)
    Now liberty at last is won,
    The dreadful dragon dead.
    'Good luck, good folk, and may the sun
    Smile on you all,' he said.
    'A brighter future lies ahead,
    So fill your days with light and be
    Forever after safe and free,
    Be happy, safe and free.'

    We seize the hour without delay:
    We all have work to do.
    We strip the thatch, we clear the clay,
    We tear the wood from view.
    We start to make our land anew,
    And forge towards our destiny:
    Forever after safe and free,
    So happy, safe and free.

    With brick and steel we build things fast,
    And build with hopeful eyes:
    Cathedrals grand and factories vast,
    With chimneys to the skies.
    The fire within us never dies
    To build a place where we can be
    Forever after safe and free,
    So happy, safe and free.

A town arises from the ground:
No more a village, slight.
We make new means to move around
And heat our homes at night,
To feed us and to give us light,
So that, enlightened, we might be
Forever after safe and free,
So happy, safe and free.

Now peace prevails throughout the land
And sunlight fills the air.
Beneath their blood-born banner stand
A folk now free from fear.
And, happy ever after here,
This nation marches on
And sings this glorious triumph-song
And flies its flag for all to see:
Forever after safe and free
So happy, safe and free!

*The scene shifts to* **Charles** *and* **Elsa***'s cottage: a medieval hovel transformed into a Victorian home. But while the fixtures and fittings have modernised, indeed, the layout is exactly the same: gas lamps stand where once the candles were, where the fireplace was there now sits a rather menacing-looking stove, etc.*

**Charles** *stands alone in the kitchen, in the process of preparing a partridge pie: a pie dish, a pastry crust and a plucked fowl sit on the table in front of him, and he reads aloud to himself the instructions from a Victorian-style recipe book:*

**Charles** (*reading*) 'As with the commander of an army or the loader of any enterprise, so it is with the maker of a pie: all lies in the preparation. Thus, having achieved your pastry crust . . .' (*He lowers the book and examines the crust, pleased with himself.*) Pastry crust achieved, and admirably. (*Reading again.*) 'Joint carefully the fowl with . . .' Joint carefully? Right, where's the . . .? (*He puts the book down, turns, and rifles through a drawer.*)

*The door opens and* **George** *strides through it.*

**Charles** (*still rifling, not seeing* **George**)   Ah, Elsa, good, you're
home, you can help me: you see, it says 'Joint carefully the
fowl,' but I can't find the –

**George** *draws his sword and lops the fowl in half.*

**Charles**   Knife. (*Turning and seeing* **George**.) Sir George!
Thank heavens you're back.

**George** (*embracing* **Charles**)   Oh, Charles, my friend: it's
good to be home!

**Charles**   Or I suppose I ought to say 'Saint George'.

**George**   Oh, you've heard?

**Charles**   We did try to reach you, George, but –

**George**   Yes: Saint George. A far cry, indeed, from the
frightened young lad who stood right here in his muddy boots
and his tattered tunic a year ago. It feels like a lifetime has
passed since that day. But, Saint George it is. I couldn't very
well have slain all those dragons in my pots and pans, now,
could I? And this cross of ours has rather caught on, too,
in fact –

**Charles**   And that's all excellent, George, but –

**George** (*displaying a medal he's wearing*)   They gave me this
medal, you know, for slaying the very last dragon. Oh, you
ought to have seen me, Charles: he was vast, savage, cunning
as you like, but I distracted him with loud noises, stunned him
with gunpowder, then captured him in a net and slayed him on
the spot! 'Distract, stun, capture', it's become something of a
signature move of mine.

**Charles**   But the thing is, George –

**George** (*gazing around the room*)   And just look at what you've
done while I've been away! Look at this place! These lights,
glowing so bright, yet not a drop of wax to be seen! This
water, clear as the morning! This –

*He stops in front of a mangle.*

Whatever on Earth this thing is: it's wonderful! You've done it, haven't you, Charles?

**Charles**   Well I'm not sure I'd say –

**George**   So where's Elsa?

**Charles**   Oh, well, she's at her work, in the manufactory.

**George**   'The manufactory': even the very name of it stirs the soul! (*Seeing the pie crust.*) And what's this?

**Charles**   A pie, George –

**George**   You're preparing her supper, I see: well, allow me.

**Charles**   George –

**George** (*roughly assembling the pie*)   So many new terms to learn, so many new skills to master, but worry not, Charles, I will tackle them all: I am back now, at last, I've retired, I'm home for good, and this pie is merely the first step on the path to my bright new future –

**Charles**   George! Please! For heaven's sake! Just put the pie down and listen to me now!

**George** *puts the pie down.*

**Charles**   I see that you're glad to be home, and *I'm* glad of it too, but there is something you really must –

**Healer's Daughter**, *a Victorian-style nurse, rushes in.*

**Healer's Daughter** (*not seeing* **George**)   Charles, Charles, I need cloth, something strong, something I can tie, some fabric, a curtain, anything, right away!

**Charles**   I – What's happened?

**Healer's Daughter**   There's been a dreadful accident, the little boy's injured his leg, we need anything you have, anything –

*She turns and sees* **George**.

**Healer's Daughter**   George! Oh, thank goodness, George: you're back!

**Charles** (*giving her a tablecloth*)    Will this do?

**Healer's Daughter** (*taking the tablecloth*)    Thank you, Charles.

**Charles**    I'll fetch him my walking stick, too.

**Healer's Daughter**    Yes, good idea. (*To* **George**.) Oh, thank heavens you're back, we need you, sir. We really need your help.

**George**    Whatever I can do.

**Charles** (*searching*)    Oh, I can't find the confounded thing! This blasted kitchen!

**George** (*to* **Healer's Daughter**)    You run on ahead, miss.

**Healer's Daughter**    Yes, sir.

*She runs out.*

**Charles** (*finding the stick*)    Here it is! (*Giving the stick to* **George**.) Quickly, take it.

**George** (*taking the stick*)    What was it you wanted to say to me, Charles?

**Charles**    It can wait: just you make sure the boy's all right.

**George**    I will, Charles. I will. Don't worry: all will be well!

*He runs out.* **Charles** *stares anxiously after him.*


### Chapter IV
IN WHICH THE MUCH-ANTICIPATED REUNION IS THWARTED

*A street crowded with nineteenth-century buildings: a printing press, a town hall, a factory etc.* **The Boy**, *in rags, is on the ground, his leg stretched out and bleeding.* **Brewer**, *a Victorian innkeeper, is supporting him, so he can sit up.* **Smith**, *a Victorian inventor, stands at a slight distance, flustered and anxious.* **The Boy** *screams.*

**Smith**    Oh goodness, where is she?

**Brewer**   Don't worry, lad: I've called for help: she's on her way.

**Boy**   No, let me up! Let me up!

**Smith**   What's he saying, there? 'Let me up'?

**Boy**   I'm fine, mister, honestly!

*The **Boy** tries to stand. He can't. He screams.*

**Brewer**   You're staying here, boy.

**Smith**   He's worried about his wages, I'll bet.

*The **Boy** struggles and screams again. **Mr** and **Mrs Butcher**, Victorian butchers, approach.*

**Mrs Butcher**   What's all this? Butcher and I were out in the slaughter-yard, we heard all the screaming, what's happened?

**Smith**   Spinning machine chewed him right up, it did: he slipped under the frames and his leg got caught in the cogs.

**Mrs Butcher**   Oh, monstrous! He won't lose it, will he?

**Boy**   I don't want to lose it, I can't lose it.

**Mrs Butcher**   Well, we can't just stand here, can we, Butcher? We have to do something!

**Smith**   Do what?

**Mrs Butcher**   I don't know: let's move him!

**Brewer**   Move him? Why?

**Mrs Butcher**   Well, we've got to do something! Come on, Butcher.

***Mr** and **Mrs Butcher** try to move the **Boy**, but he screams.*

**Smith**   Oh, no, please, stop! You're hurting him!

***Crier** arrives, a Victorian printer, covered in ink.*

**Crier**   What on Earth's happening, sirs? I heard you all the way from the press!

**Smith**    The lad's little leg got chewed in the gearing, Crier. Oh goodness.

**Crier**    Oh, not another one: please! Where's Healer?

**Brewer**    She's coming: she was up at the miners' cottages: one of the shafts fell in this morning.

**Boy**    It's bleeding lots! She needs to get here quick!

**Mrs Butcher**    We've tried moving him!

**Crier**    Moving him?! For what purpose did you move him, madam?!

**Mrs Butcher**    Well, we had to do something!

**Crier**    Let me have a look there, son.

**Smith**    It's bad, sir, oh, it's bad, I know it is: the scream he gave when it caught him, oh, it was like nothing else in the world, like a long loud crunch but very high.

**Crier** *raises the* **Boy***'s trouser leg and winces.*

**Crier**    Oh, that's . . . that's mashed him up good and proper.

**Brewer**    I've had quite enough of this: one of the other piecers lost three of his fingers last week, I heard he might lose the arm.

**Smith**    I've said it myself, sir, I said to my wife, I said it's running far too fast, I said –

**Healer**, *a Victorian nurse, runs in, having just washed her hands.*

**Smith**    Oh, Healer, thank goodness, please do something!

**Mrs Butcher**    She will, Smith, she will.

**Healer**    I was all the way up at the cottages: what on Earth's happened?

**Boy**    It hurts!

**Healer** (*checking the wound*)    Oh my.

**Boy**    What is it? Is it bad?

**Mrs Butcher** (*to* **Mr Butcher**)   He'll be out for a week.

**Healer**   For a month.

**Boy**   No, please, missus: I'll lose my post if I don't get back soon, they'll give it to another lad!

**Driver**, *a Victorian draywoman, arrives, drunk, but hiding it.*

**Driver**   What's all this? What's happened?

**Brewer**   Where've you been? You were due at the inn with my barrels this morning!

**Crier**   Accident at the factory: lad caught his leg.

**Healer**   It could've been much worse.

**Smith**   Oh, thank goodness Elsa pulled the lever and stopped the machine or it would've swallowed him whole!

**Driver**   Elsa did what?!

**Crier**   Oh heavens: she's done for!

**Smith**   What? But she saved the little lad!

**Crier**   You remember what happened to Draper? His wife's giving birth and he tells the knocker-upper, but he still gets put from his post and loses his cottage, and him and his wife and the baby are out on the street, and all because he's half an hour late! And Elsa just shut the whole damned factory down: she's done for, I say!

*The* **Boy** *screams.*

**Healer**   We need to clean the wound.

**Driver** (*handing* **Healer** *a hip-flask filled with gin*)   Here, use this.

**Brewer**   You're paid to deliver the gin, Driver, not drink it.

**Driver**   It's medicinal.

**Mrs Butcher** (*nudging* **Mr Butcher**)   Didn't I tell you –

**Driver**   How I choose to get through my day is no business of yours, madam.

**Smith**   It's all my fault.

**Crier**   It isn't you, Smith, it's him: he's the one flogging us onwards, with no thought to our safety at all!

**Brewer**   But a little boy?

**Healer**   You'd shudder if I told you how many I see in a month: arms, legs, all chewed up.

**Mrs Butcher** (*angry, emotional*)   Oh, it's all chewed up in this wretched place, isn't it, Butcher? Day into night, air into smoke, men, women and children all chewed up and limbless, homeless, filthy, starving –

**Mr Butcher** (*soothing*)   It's all right, Butcher. There, there.

**Healer's Daughter** *arrives, with the ripped-up tablecloth, as bandages.*

**Healer's Daughter**   Bandages, Mother!

**Healer** (*taking them, getting to work*)   Thank heavens.

**Brewer** (*to the* **Boy**)   Hold on there, lad: it's nearly over.

**Healer's Daughter** (*to* **Healer**)   George is back, he's back!

**Crier**   What?!

**Driver**   George?!

**Healer's Daughter**   I saw him a moment ago, at Charles's cottage. He's on his way here.

**Smith**   Oh, thank goodness!

**Mrs Butcher**   Did you hear that, Butcher? George is back!

**Healer** (*to the* **Boy**)   How's that, then, lad?

**Crier**   Not a moment too soon, if you ask me!

**George** *arrives.*

**Driver**   George!

**Brewer**   George!

**Mrs Butcher**   Thank heavens!

**Smith**   You're truly here!

**George**   Courtesy of Charles: a walking stick. How's the lad? Is everything all right?

**Healer**   The worst of it's over. He won't lose the leg, at least.

**George** (*to the* **Boy**)   How are you, boy?

**Boy**   Glad to see you, George.

*He hugs* **George**.

**George**   What happened here?

**Boy**   The machine.

**Smith**   See, I made a machine to spin cotton, sir, a spinning machine, I suppose –

**George**   A machine to spin cotton?

**Smith**   Yes, sir, I –

**George**   A machine to spin cotton! Just look at this place: giant turrets, spewing smoke into the sky; proud, grand buildings, fit for the ages; new rivers, cut by men, right into land, to ferry your goods all over the isle; bridges the size of which I've never seen, and I saw this thing thundering along one of them, as if of itself, carrying folk and making a sound, like some great bird, what in the name of wonder was that thing?!

**Brewer**   It's called a locomotive, George, but –

**George**   Though this place is small, we are yet mighty, it's –

*He sees the folk's faces, and stops.*

What? What's the matter? Why are you looking at me like that?

**Driver**   You really don't know, sir, do you?

**Healer**   Did nobody tell you?

**George**   Did nobody tell me what?

**Mrs Butcher**    He's back, George.

**George**    Who?

**Crier**    The Dragon's back.

**George**    No. What? He can't be.

**Driver**    Not at first, he wasn't.

**Brewer**    No, not at first.

**Healer's Daughter**    At first, everything was wonderful.

**Crier**    We did just as you said, sir.

**Healer**    We built and we built, just as you said.

**Brewer**    And we took what we could from the land, and we started to trade it.

**Boy**    Cloth, George!

**Driver**    And coal, sir. So much coal.

**Smith**    And we made new machines to spin the cloth and dig out the coal.

**Brewer**    But the machines, they *ran* on coal.

**Healer**    So that meant we needed more coal, sir.

**Healer's Daughter**    More and more.

**Boy**    More and more.

**Mrs Butcher**    And we traded the things we'd made for things from abroad.

**Crier**    Food.

**Mrs Butcher**    And fine fabrics.

**Mr Butcher**    More and more.

**Boy**    More and more.

**Driver**    And we had to make sure we could keep what we wanted to keep.

**Smith**   So we wrote laws and statutes.

**Healer**   And organised the money and the property.

**Brewer**   And soon it was all just one big system.

**Healer's Daughter**   A system we couldn't stop.

**Crier**   That just kept grinding, on and on.

**Driver**   On and on.

**Boy**   More and more.

**Smith**   And then he was –

*The door of the town hall flies open, and the* **Dragon** *is there, smartly dressed in top hat and tails.*

**Dragon**   And then I was back.

*He emerges, flanked by four guards, one of whom bears a glowing casket.*

You know, I was so lonely after you killed me, George. Just stray shards of matter, carried on the wind. But then they embarked on this great project of theirs, and slowly, very slowly, I could feel myself starting to stir. And as they began to worship, more and more, at the altar of efficiency, of productivity, I began to jerk back into life. It was almost as if they'd summoned me: a system needs a master, after all: someone to fashion the forces of production; someone to place each man, woman and child on the great assembly line of progress. Someone like me.

**George**   I've vanquished you before, sir: I'll vanquish you again.

*He draws his sword and charges at the* **Dragon***. One of the guards steps in front of* **George** *and knocks him down with his rifle butt.*

**Dragon**   Oh no, George, you see: it just doesn't work like that any more. This form you see standing in front of you isn't the real me. It's not a thing to be slashed or stabbed: it's just a convenience I use when occasion demands it. I am not in *here*, George: I'm out there.

*As he speaks he opens the casket and removes and unfolds a beautiful blueprint of the island.*

I am timetables and ledgers, graphs and diagrams. I am wages and charges, loans and fines. I am lists and charts and reasons and rules. I am science and logic and incontrovertible fact. I am the end of the argument and the beginning of silence. My fire is now a blast furnace, my roar is now the roar of the mill, and my spikes are the spokes of the vast machine that grinds and chews and pounds and strains and slams night after day, day after night, forever and forever and forever.

*He slams the casket shut.*

And my word is the law.

*The door of the factory flies open and* **Elsa***, hands chained, is there.*

**Elsa**   George!

**George**   Elsa!

**Pike** *and* **Son** *emerge behind* **Elsa***, escorting her. The* **Millers** *and the* **Fielders** *also filter into the street.*

**Dragon**   This woman has made a gross attack on me today: she has halted the work in my factory, a crime I account the foulest in the land. And thus, at noon tomorrow, George, your darling Elsa will hang. (*To* **Pike** *and* **Son***.*) Take her away.

**Pike** *and* **Son** *begin to lead* **Elsa** *off. The* **Dragon** *strolls back to the hall.*

**Elsa**   I'm sorry, George, I truly am –

**George**   Elsa, fear not –

**Dragon**   Remove her!

*And* **Elsa** *is gone. The* **Dragon** *reaches the door of the hall, opens it, turns, and raises his hat.*

**Dragon**   Welcome home, Saint George.

*The* **Dragon** *goes inside the hall, followed by the guards.*

**Smith**   I'm sorry, George.

**Healer**   We all are, sir.

**Mrs Butcher**   We never intended for this to happen, sir!

**George**   It is no fault of yours, my friends. Yet Elsa will not hang tomorrow, you mark my words. I have a plan, but it requires your help. Smith, we'll need all the weapons you can muster.

**Smith**   Yes, George.

**George**   Does anyone here have access to explosives?

**Alice**   I've got some at home.

**Amy**   You what?

**Ann**   Alice!

**Alice** (*to* **Ann**)   I swiped them from the mine.

**George**   Excellent: fetch them, and meet me, at Charles's cottage. (*To the* **Boy**.) Come, boy: let's get you away.

*He goes, helping the* **Boy**. *The folk begin to follow.*

**Ann**   Alice, what've I told you about stealing?

**Amy**   Explosives, Alice? Why?

**Alice**   Not sure: just thought they might come in useful, I suppose.

**Amy**   Well, now they have. Well done.

**Alice**   Thank you, Amy.

**Ann**   Let's go.

**Miller** *and* **Young Miller** *are the last to leave.* **Young Miller** *turns to look at the hall.*

**Young Miller**   The, the, the, the, the, the, the –

**Miller**   Peace, my boy. Peace now. George is back. Our troubles are nearly over.

*She leads him off.*

**Chapter V**
IN WHICH TWO OLD FOES ARE THROWN TOGETHER

*The town prison, a little while later. In a damp, cramped, stone-built cell sits* **Henry**, *on his cot. He is dirty, dishevelled and haggard-looking, and his clothes are in rags. Next to him on the cot sits Pike's* **Son**, *a prison guard. Pike's* **Son** *holds a ragged notebook, from which* **Henry** *is teaching him to read.*

**Son** (*spelling it out, slowly*) 'Wha . . . What . . . warms . . . a . . . man . . . mo . . . mo . . . more?'

**Henry**    Yes, good.

**Son**    'Than . . . a . . . fire? What enri . . . enri . . .'

**Henry**    Break it down into parts, like I showed you.

**Son**    'Enri-ches . . . enriches . . .'

**Henry**    Good.

**Son**    'A man . . . more . . . than gold?'

**Henry**    Yes.

**Son**    'What endu . . . endures . . . thou . . . though . . . it never . . . grows . . . tired? What ag . . . ag . . .' Oh, I can't do it, sir. I can't.

**Henry**    Come on, lad. Remember why you're practising.

**Son** (*like a catechism*)    I want to write a letter to the Healer's Daughter, and –

**Son** *and* **Henry**    Tell her she's the loveliest creature I've / you've ever seen.

**Henry**    Precisely. So we need to keep on with it, then, if we wish to tackle such complex things as love letters.

**Son**    Right. Yes, sir. 'What ag . . . ages?'

**Henry**    Good!

**Son**    'Ages but never gets old.' I did it! 'What warms a man more than a fire? What enriches a man more than gold? What endures, though it never grows tired? What ages, but never gets old?'

**Henry**   Excellent, lad.

**Pike** (*off*)   Son! Where are you? Are you there, son!

**Son** (*calling out, sheepish*)   Yes, Father.

**Pike** *looks into the cell.*

**Pike**   There you are: what are you doing? I've told you not to sit in there with him!

**Son**   But he's teaching me to read, Father!

**Pike**   I don't care if he's teaching you to play the fiddle blindfolded: he's a dangerous criminal, and he's not to be fraternised with!

**Son** (*standing*)   Yes, Father. Sorry, Father.

**Pike**   Will you go and let the debtors out? It's time for their evening breath of air.

**Son**   Yes, Father.

**Pike** (*to* **Henry**)   And as for you, sir, I am warning you: keep away from my son!

*He goes.*

**Son**   I'd best be off, then, sir.

**Henry**   Indeed.

*Pike's* **Son** *makes to go, but then stops, and turns.*

**Son**   Oh, sir, if you don't mind my asking: what is it?

**Henry**   What's what, boy?

**Son**   'What warms a man more than a fire?'

**Henry**   Friendship.

**Son**   Oh. (*Awkwardly.*) Good night, then, sir.

*He goes.* **Henry** *sits.* **Pike** *leads* **Elsa** *on, and brings her to the adjoining cell to* **Henry**'s.

**Pike** (*to* **Elsa**)    Here you go: there's a cot in the corner with a blanket if you want it, and a bucket for, you know, a bucket. (*He shakes his head.*) I'm awfully sorry to put you in here next to him, miss, but the prison's stuffed to the brim at the moment. But there's nothing doing now, I suppose, so you'd best try and get some sleep.

*He starts to go.*

**Elsa**    Thank you, Pike.

**Henry** *starts, hearing* **Elsa**'s *voice.* **Pike** *nods to* **Elsa**, *and goes. Silence.* **Elsa** *goes over to the cot and sits on it.*

**Henry**    Elsa!

*Silence.*

Elsa, it's me! It's Henry!

*Silence.*

You know: Henry –

**Elsa**    I know it's you, Henry.

**Henry**    Oh, Elsa, thank goodness, I –

**Elsa**    If we're going to be stuck here together, sir, we ought to establish a rule: we do not speak to one another.

**Henry**    But I –

**Elsa**    Did you not hear me, sir?! Silence!

*Silence.*

**Henry**    But please, Elsa, just let me speak to you, just for a moment, I beg you –

**Elsa** (*speaking over him*)    I don't want to hear it, Henry –

**Henry** (*speaking over her*)    I was there, at my window, watching –

**Elsa** (*speaking over him*)    I'm not listening to you –

**Henry** (*speaking over her*)    And I saw it, Elsa, everything that happened –

**Elsa** (*speaking over him*)   Henry, please –

**Henry** (*loud*)   I saw it all!

**Elsa** *stops speaking.*

**Henry**   And I'm so, so sorry.

*Silence.*

I saw George come back. I saw the Dragon. I saw you being marched from the factory. What on Earth did you do?

*Silence.*

Elsa?

**Elsa**   I stopped the machine.

**Henry**   What?

**Elsa**   The little boy's leg got caught in the gears so I pulled the lever and stopped it.

**Henry**   That's all?

**Elsa**   Well that's enough, these days: he just had Weaver up on the gallows for breaking a shuttle, before that it was Shearer he hanged.

**Henry**   What did he do?

**Elsa**   Over-stoked the furnace in the mill, half near burned the whole thing down. They had to close the place for three days afterwards. The Dragon was incensed. Show of strength, I'm guessing.

**Henry** (*working it out*)   No, it isn't strength, Elsa, it's, oh heavens, that's how you do it, isn't it?

**Elsa**   What are you talking about, Henry?

**Henry**   I think I know how to beat him, Elsa. I think I know how to defeat the Dragon! You have to let me help!

**Elsa**   We don't want your help, Henry.

**Henry**   But I know the Dragon better than anyone, Elsa. Please, just listen to me now. I'm asking you to trust me.

**Elsa**   And why on Earth should I do that? You aided the Dragon for years, Henry: trotting along after him in your livery like a lovesick dog. You were his closest ally. So why should I listen to a single thing you say?

**Henry**   Because I hated it! Because I hated every moment of my wretched, servile life. Because I woke up every morning sick to my stomach with the thought of the day ahead. Because the rush of pure relief I felt when he died is the only true happiness I've ever known in my life.

**Elsa**   Oh, nonsense, Henry.

**Henry**   What?

**Elsa**   Nonsense! You made your choice when we were children: don't pretend that you didn't.

**Henry**   I went into my father's trade, just as Crier went into his, just as you went into yours. If I'd refused he'd have killed me: follow the Dragon or die: that was my choice. And so I followed him.

**Elsa**   But you didn't have to enjoy yourself quite so much while you were doing it, did you? We all saw you, Henry: lovingly turning the words as you heralded his entrance; the look in your eyes as you carted folk off to be killed. You were having fun, sir.

**Henry**   And is it any wonder, given how vicious you all were to me? The footman's son: I was practically branded from birth. You recall when we were children, Elsa: not a day went by when I wasn't half-drowned in a horse trough, or smeared all over with the filth of some bedpan or other.

**Elsa**   Oh, please, Henry –

**Henry**   And d'you remember my cat, Elsa? A lovely little house cat, small and black and gentle and soft like velvet; my mother bought him for me: I loved that cat. And d'you remember Tanner, Elsa? He tied a string of rusty nails to its tail. The poor thing scratched itself to pieces trying to get away from those nails, Tanner tortured my cat, Elsa!

**Elsa**   And then you and the Dragon incinerated him for it afterwards.

**Henry**   The Dragon incinerated him, Elsa. Not me. And not for that.

**Elsa**   So it was merely coincidence, was it, that all the boys who bullied you ended up dead?

**Henry**   I did things, yes, and I'm sorry. But people did things to me too. And now the only person who was ever nice to me won't even listen when I'm trying to tell her I've changed.

**Elsa**   The Dragon was nice to you, Henry. Why don't you slink back to him?

**Henry**   D'you think I couldn't do that, if I wanted to? D'you think he doesn't come and stand, right there, outside my window, every day, and beckon me back? I could be free of this place in a second if that's what I wanted. I'd leave this miserable, lonely hole for good, and be back at my post. He'd give me a house, a big one, a bed, clean sheets, decent clothes, edible food, wages, respect –

**Elsa**   Then why don't you go to him?

**Henry**   Because that isn't what I want. I want what you have, Elsa. I want to feel like a part of the place where I was born. And doesn't the fact that I want that so much more than warmth or houses or gold show you I'm serious?

**Elsa**   No, Henry. It doesn't. And nothing ever will. So why don't you write to your precious dragon and tell him you're coming back to his side? Because we don't want you on ours. Good night to you, sir.

**Henry**   Elsa, I –

**Elsa**   Good night!

*She lies down and covers herself with a blanket.* **Henry** *sits, in silence. A thought begins to dawn on him. He stands and goes to pick up his notebook. He finds a pencil, and begins to write. He stops, tears out the page, folds it, writes a name on the front, and goes to the cell door.*

**Henry** (*whispering*)   Boy! Boy!

*Pike's* **Son** *arrives.*

**Son**   Yes, sir?

**Henry**   Deliver this note at once.

**Son**   Yes, sir.

*He takes the note.*

**Henry**   And you're not to practise your reading on this one. It's private.

**Son**   Sir.

**Son** *goes.* **Henry** *stands.*


## Chapter VI
IN WHICH A PLAN IS BORN

**Charles** *and* **Elsa***'s cottage, the middle of the night.* **George** *and the townsfolk are all crammed into* **Charles***'s cramped kitchen, using everything available as seating (the few chairs themselves, the kitchen table, the floor etc.).* **George** *stands facing the seated townsfolk and, with the aid of a large blackboard, upon which is a crudely drawn aerial view of the town square, takes them through his plan of attack, in a distinctly militaristic manner.*

**George**   Thus: as the clock begins to strike noon, Elsa shall be marched from the prison, hence – (*Points.*) to the gallows, hither – (*Points.*) The Dragon will position himself here – (*Points.*) where he will stand, flanked by his entourage of four – am I correct in thinking four?

**Crier**   Four.

**George**    Four guards. Now, you townsfolk shall form the
crowd, gathered in front of the scaffold here – (*Points.*) and I will
conceal myself here – (*Points.*) and, at the appropriate juncture,
will join the very back of the crowd here – (*Points.*) disguised,
naturally, so as not to give up our enterprise. Thus, when you
see Mr Pike's hand go to the lever, we distract – (*Points to a
group of townsfolk, who put up their hands.*) stun – (*Another group put
up their hands.*) and capture – (*Another group put up their hands.*) at
which point I, George, shall rush forward with my dagger and
slay the Dragon.

**Ann Fielder**    Sorry, how will we know when exactly we're
meant to stun the guards?

**George**    You'll know because the guards will be distracted,
by the distraction.

**Amy Fielder**    Are you going to give us a signal, sir?

**George**    No, since I will be at the back, here, and you will be
facing in this direction –

**Alice Fielder**    In what direction?

**George**    Look: a simple rehearsal will reveal the elegance of
the plan. I'll conceal myself outside, whilst you begin at the
beginning. Mr Brewer, if you please.

*He goes.*

**Brewer**    Very well, erm . . . Let's begin at the beginning.

**Mrs Butcher**    Yes, so when I see Mr Pike reach for the
lever, I shout to go.

**Healer**    What will you shout?

**Mrs Butcher**    I thought perhaps simply a straightforward
'Go!'

**Healer**    Right.

**Miller**    Yes, then we bang our pots and pans at the front of
the crowd.

**Healer's Daughter**    And we're banging at the rear of the crowd.

**Ann Fielder**    So we reach into our pockets and retrieve the explosives.

**Alice Fielder**    And then we throw them to the ground.

**Amy Fielder**    Throw or drop?

**Alice Fielder**    Throw them. Like this –

*She throws a pouch to the floor and it explodes, emitting a loud BANG.*

**Amy Fielder**    What d'you do that for?!

**Alice Fielder**    You asked if it was throw or drop.

**Ann Fielder**    The point is we throw them and it stuns the guards.

**Amy Fielder**    Which we'll just take for granted from now on.

**Brewer**    Meanwhile, we have been readying our weapons.

**Driver**    Where are the weapons?

**Brewer**    Smith's bringing them.

**Charles**    So we ready our weapons.

**Driver**    Then once the bangs go off – I run at the first guard.

**Charles**    I run at the second guard.

**Brewer**    I run at the third.

*Silence.*

**Mrs Butcher**    Look sharp, Butcher, this is your bit.

**Mr Butcher** (*quietly*)    But this isn't going to work.

**Mrs Butcher**    What's that you're saying?

**Mr Butcher**    I'm just saying I don't think this is going to work –

**Mrs Butcher** (*angry*)   Oh, for goodness' sake: you're embarrassing yourself!

**Driver**   Wait: let him have his say. Go on, Mr Butcher.

**Mr Butcher**   Yes, all this distracting and stunning and capturing is all very well and good, but it's not going to get us anywhere, is it?

**Healer**   You've forgotten the bit where George runs in and stabs him.

**Mr Butcher**   Stabs him, though?

**Healer**   Yes.

**Mr Butcher**   As in, stabs him with a knife?

**Healer**   Exactly.

**Mr Butcher**   But, with respect, we've tried that before, and it just didn't work, did it?

**Healer**   Well, no. No it didn't.

**Mr Butcher**   I mean, the Dragon's different, isn't he? So perhaps we need to, you know, be different too.

*Silence.*

Do you follow, Mrs Butcher?

**Mrs Butcher**   Yes, I think I do.

**George** *bursts in.*

**George**   At which point I, George, shall rush forward with my dagger, stab the Dragon, and free the town for good.

*Silence.*

Apologies, I . . . Am I early?

*Silence.*

What is it?

**Mrs Butcher**   Forgive us, sir, but we have a number of concerns about your plan.

**George**  What are you talking about, madam? 'Distract, stun, capture,' I've vanquished countless dragons in precisely this manner.

**Mrs Butcher**  But this one isn't like those ones, sir, if you catch my meaning. He's not something to be stabbed or slashed.

**George**  And whyever not?

**Mrs Butcher**  Because we've tried it before and it didn't work. Tell him, Crier.

**Crier**  There was a fellow a few months back, name of Cutter, loses his wife and his daughter to the black lung, so he tracks the Dragon down, and shoots him at point-blank range with a flintlock pistol. The bullet, sir, it bounces right off him. There were scores of witnesses standing, amazed; and the Dragon just smiles, then tips his hat and walks away.

**George**  With respect, Crier, I am not a disgruntled clothmaker. I am Saint George the Dragon-slayer: I know what I'm doing.

**Driver**  But with equal respect, George: you don't, not this time around. He's not a big hulking lump of dragon-flesh any more: that body of his isn't even real. He's unkillable, sir.

**George**  Have you quite forgot me, madam? Killing unkillable dragons is quite literally my profession! Did you not see me last year, plunging a dagger into his skull as I twirled gracefully through the sky?! Through the sky, madam!

**Driver**  No, of course, I –

**George**  (*showing his medal*)  Well, perhaps this medal will convince you, then: there, have a look at the inscription: 'For killing the unkillable –'

**Brewer**  George, you're the pride of this nation, and your deeds have made us famous throughout the world, but this is no longer the land that you left, and he is no longer the dragon you killed. We are your countrymen, George, and you are our champion, but we're begging you, sir, please do not lead us into a fight we cannot win.

**Smith** *enters, with a large box of weapons.*

**Smith**   So what I've done here is I've gathered all the small hand-held weapons I could find, so I've got your short swords and your cutlasses, your clubs and the like, but my wife, she said, 'There's not enough in there, you'll need twice that and more,' so I said, 'Well, they can share, can't they?' and she said, 'What d'you mean: one sword between two?!' 'No, I didn't mean the sword, woman!' 'Well there's no need to be sharp.' 'I'm not being sharp, I'm just –' Where you going, come back, I –

*He stops.*

What? What is it? I mean, she's a lovely woman, but –

**George**   You can put the weapons down, Smith.

**Smith**   So no swords, then?

**George** (*rubbing*)   No, and no cutlasses, or maces, or stunning, or capturing, or distracting or anything of the sort.

**Amy**   We're giving up?

**Charles**   Might I remind you, sir, that my daughter is due to hang tomorrow –

**George**   And I made a solemn pledge that I would save her. But we're dealing with a different kind of dragon here, so we need a different kind of plan.

**Boy**   I knew he wouldn't let us down!

**George**   So you must teach me now.

**Alice**   Us teach you, sir?

**George**   How do we kill this monster?

**Brewer**   Well, attacks on his person are out.

**George**   So where does he get his strength from, then?

**Crier**   From the army, sir. He sends them in on the slimmest of pretexts.

**Healer**   We can't kill the entire army, Crier!

**Alice**   I do have quite a lot of explosives, actually.

**Ann**   Alice!

**Alice**   You got any better ideas?

**Ann**   I –

**Alice**   Didn't think so.

**George**   So let's assume we can't explode the army, then.

**Healer's Daughter**   We could petition him for clemency!

**George** (*writing it down*)   Petitioning.

**Smith**   Yes, my wife, sir, she's grown rather close to the sister of a certain magistrate, and if we could somehow get him to grant us an audience –

**Mrs Butcher**   You think we're going to defeat the Dragon by having a chat with a magistrate?

**Smith**   Well, he's a very powerful man and –

**Miller**   We're not going to petition the Dragon out of existence, Smith.

**George** (*rubbing it out*)   So, moving on from petitioning, any other ideas? Areas of weakness, perhaps?

**Mrs Butcher**   He's quite vain.

**George** (*writing*)   Quite vain. (*Rubbing out.*) No, I'm rubbing that one out immediately.

**Driver**   Quite vain?

**Mrs Butcher**   Oh go back to your hip-flask, Driver.

**George**   What else? What does he love the most in the world? What does he covet?

**Healer**   I don't follow you, sir.

**George**   Well, he's still a dragon, isn't he? So what does he hoard?

**Healer's Daughter**   Money, sir. Wealth.

**George** (*writing*)   Attack the hoard. And what is the source of it?

**Crier**   Well, it's us, sir. It's all the mining and weaving and spinning and milling. It's made him as rich as an emperor.

**George**   Good, so –

**Miller**   So we could just stop, then, couldn't we? Refuse to do it any more. If we abandon our posts at the mill, and you – (*To the* **Boy**.) do the same at the mine, and you – (*To* **Driver**.) set down your cart, then –

**Brewer**   But there are plenty of folk out of work, Miller. I should know, they're my best customers. You abandon your post and he'll have someone in to fill it before you know it.

**Driver**   Well maybe some of us care more about beating this monster than we do about our takings.

**Mrs Butcher**   Oh come on now, Driver –

**Driver**   And look who's leaping to his defence, the woman in the lovely brocade dress: how much did that cost then, eh?

**George**   Please! Might we return to the matter at hand?! If we can't explode the army or petition a magistrate, or diminish his resources, then how exactly do we defeat this dragon?

**Young Miller**   I, I, I, I, I –

**Miller**   Peace, now, boy. Shhh.

**Young Miller**   I, I, I, I know him.

**Alice**   He's trying to speak.

**Young Miller**   I . . . know him.

**Mrs Butcher**   He does and all, Miller: he wants to speak.

**Young Miller**    I . . . know.

**Mrs Butcher**    'I know him,' he's saying!

**Crier**    Listen!

**Miller** (*amazed*)    Go on, son.

**Young Miller**    When I was small, in the cave, the monster burned himself on me.

*He points to a large burn, across his face and neck.*

I used to wake up screaming. Every night. I thought I was dead. And when you killed him George . . .

**Miller**    The dreams stopped, didn't they, son? For a while.

**Young Miller**    But now he's back stronger than before, buried deep, deep in everything. In everything. I know him. He's out there, and he's laughing and laughing and laughing.

*Silence.*

**Charles**    The lad's right, George.

*Silence.*

Thank you all for coming. I appreciate your efforts here tonight. But this isn't a battle we can win. And so I cannot ask you to fight it.

**George**    But what about Elsa, Charles?

**Charles**    He's right, George: it's suicide. It will be the end of us all.

**Boy**    But he's going to hang her, Charles!

**Charles**    My daughter is no fool, boy. She'll understand. (*To everyone.*) Now, if you wouldn't mind helping me with the chairs.

*Silence. The townsfolk slowly begin to filter out.*

**Brewer**    We'll still be there tomorrow, Charles. All of us.

**Smith**    And I could still see about that magistrate, if you like?

**Charles**   It's all right, Smith.

**Healer's Daughter** (*at the door*)   Are you coming, Mother?

**Healer** (*going to the* **Boy**)   Best give his leg the once-over.

*Silence.* **Charles** *goes over to the stove.* **Healer** *and* **Daughter** *start to examine the* **Boy***'s leg.* **George** *sits.*

**George** (*standing*)   Pass me my sword.

**Charles**   What?

**George**   Pass me my sword, Charles: I won't just sit here, I cannot.

**Boy**   Yes! I knew it!

**Charles**   George, the Miller's lad's right: this is precisely what he's expecting us to do.

**George** (*to* **Charles**)   Which way is the prison?

**Charles** (*confiscating* **George***'s sword*)   He'll have his soldiers ready –

**George** (*to the* **Boy**)   Which way is the prison, boy?

**Boy**   Follow the river, the second bridge, it's on your right.

**George**   The second bridge. Give me my sword, Charles.

**Charles**   I won't.

**Boy**   Charles, he needs his sword!

**Healer**   Bed for you now, lad. Come on.

*She and her* **Daughter** *grab the* **Boy** *and move him towards the bed.*

**Boy**   But –

**George**   Charles, I am warning you –

**Healer** (*to the* **Boy**)   Shhh, let's get you to bed.

**Charles**   Don't be a fool, George.

**George**   I swore an oath: give me my sword.

**Charles**   I shan't, sir.

*Pike's* **Son** *comes through the door.*

**Son** (*running to* **George**)   George! There's a letter for you.

**George**   I've no time for letters. Charles, I will take it from you if I have to.

**Son**   No, sir, please: it's urgent.

**George**   Did you not hear me, boy? I'll read it later.

**Son**   No, now! You have to read it now. It's from the prison.

**George**   The prison?

**Son**   Yes, sir.

**George** *snatches the letter.*

**George**   Elsa!

*He reads the letter.*

**Son**   I shouldn't be here, sir. I'll need to get back.

*He rushes out, and runs into* **Healer's Daughter** *in the doorway.*

**Son**   Oh, you're on your way out too, are you? Shall I walk with you?

**Healer's Daughter**   I'd rather walk alone.

**Son**   Yes, yes, of course, I'll just –

*But she's gone. Pike's* **Son** *leaves too.* **George**'s *eyes light up.*

**Charles**   What is it, George? What's wrong?

**Healer**   Are you all right, sir?

**George**   Get everyone back here at once.

**Charles**   George?

**George**   We're going to save Elsa!

## Chapter VII
IN WHICH A PLAN IS PUT INTO ACTION

*The town square, the following morning. It is shortly before noon. Distant drums, getting closer. An imposing gallows/scaffold is erected in the square. The townsfolk slowly filter on.* **Mr** and **Mrs Butcher** *pass before the scaffold.*

**Mrs Butcher**   It's a hideous thing, that there, Mr Butcher. A wicked, hideous thing.

**Mr Butcher**   Come away now, Mrs Butcher.

*She shudders.* **Ann** and **Amy Fielder** *pass by, from the other side.*

**Amy Fielder**   She's late. Why is she late?

**Ann Fielder**   She'll be here, Amy. Don't worry.

**Amy Fielder** (*worried*)   I'm not worried.

**Crier**, **Driver** and **Smith** *pass by, from the other side.*

**Crier**   What time is it now?

**Driver**   Two minutes to noon.

**Smith**   Well, we can always rely on the Dragon to be punctual, I suppose.

**Alice** *runs on and joins* **Ann** and **Amy.**

**Alice Fielder** (*panting*)   I'm sorry, I'm sorry.

**Ann Fielder**   You've cut it fine, haven't you?

**Alice Fielder**   Well, I'm here now, aren't I?

*The clock begins to strike noon.*

**Brewer**   Right: come on!

*The townsfolk ready themselves.*

**Healer's Daughter**   Charles! You're over there!

**Charles** (*changing position*)   Ah, yes.

**Brewer**    Good luck, everyone!

**Pike** *and* **Son** *march* **Elsa** *to the gallows.* **Pike** *mounts the scaffold, with* **Elsa**, *and positions her over the trapdoor. Meanwhile, the* **Dragon** *arrives, from the hall, flanked by his guards. The* **Dragon** *mounts the scaffold, and the guards form a protective line between the* **Dragon** *and the crowd. The clock finishes striking.*

**Dragon**    Mr Crier, why don't you do the honours? For old times' sake.

**Crier**    Sir. (*Official tone.*) The prisoner here has received the capital sentence. She will hereby be hanged by the neck until she is dead.

**Dragon**    Marvellous. (*To* **Elsa**.) Any last words?

**Elsa** *is silent.*

**Dragon**    Oh, look at you: too heartbroken to speak! Where was your darling George last night, when you lay cold in your cell? No daring rescue, no audacious elopement. Nothing. And now here you stand: one pull of a lever away from your death. Let's be about the business, then. Mr Pike: you may begin.

**Pike** *puts the rope around* **Elsa**'s *neck, then goes and stands by the lever.*

**Dragon**    I think, of all my machines, this one is my very favourite. Such elegance, such delicious simplicity! A rope and a lever. That's all. Just pull, drop, snap: done. The weight of the body itself takes the life. Oh, the achieve of the thing! And so, Mr Pike, if you would.

**Pike** *puts his hand on the lever.*

**Mrs Butcher**    Go!

*The distraction begins: the banging of pots and pans from various parts of the crowd. The* **Fielder Sisters** *run forward and throw their explosives to the ground, stunning the guards.* **Crier**, **Brewer**, **Smith**, **Driver**, **Mr Butcher** *and* **Charles** *remove concealed weapons and capture the stunned guards, leaving the path to the* **Dragon** *clear. The hooded figure at the back charges forward, dagger drawn. But just before the figure reaches its target, it recoils, shoved back, as if stopped by an invisible force. The **Dragon** laughs.*

**Dragon** (*laughing*)   You fool, you utter fool, Saint George! Guards!

*The guards struggle free, then point their rifles into the crowd.*

You charge at me as if I were some hulking, scaly beast to be slain in hand-to-hand combat! So predictable. You just don't change, do you, sir? But I do. And there's a law against obstructing a public hanging. Or, if there isn't, there is now. (*To the guards.*) Gentlemen, as soon as Elsa twitches her last, do me the kindness of shooting Saint George in the head. (*To **George**.*) What do you say, sir?

*The figure removes its hood. It's **Healer**. She smiles.*

**Healer**   Dragon, I challenge you!

**Dragon**   What?!

**George** (*standing at the door of the **Dragon**'s hall, bearing the glowing casket in his arms*)   You heard the woman: Dragon, I challenge you!

**Dragon**   No, put that down!

**George**   I'll admit, you had me doubting myself. But if there's one thing I know about dragons, sir, it's this: you hunt them where they live.

*He opens the box and unfolds the beautiful blueprint.*

**Dragon**   I'm warning you, George –

**George**   Not in a body: no, you're too clever for that. But in a foul system of laws, and statutes, ledgers and plans, pulleys and gears. You may have changed your form, Dragon, but you can still be slain.

*He tears a section off the blueprint.*

**Dragon** (*wincing in pain*)   No!

**George**   We're going to crawl inside each thing that you are, and destroy it from within: we're going to root out each dark instrument that drives your power and rip it apart. I'm pulling the lever on this vast machine of yours, and banishing you back to the darkness, where you belong.

*The* **Dragon** *screams and falls to his knees. The townsfolk crowd in around him.*

**Dragon**   This is not the end, Saint George.

**Driver**   You're right, sir: it's the beginning.

**George** *makes a final, definitive tear of the blueprint, and the* **Dragon** *disappears, in a flash of green and gold light.*

**Boy**   Did we do it, George?

**George**   We did.

**Boy**   We did it, everyone!

*The townsfolk laugh and cheer.* **George** *goes over to* **Elsa**, *removes the noose from her neck, and releases her.*

**Healer's Daughter**   You were wonderful, Mother.

**Brewer**   Thank you, Healer.

**Healer**   It's quite all right, rather exciting in fact.

**Elsa**   I'll admit you had me worried, there, for a moment, George.

**George**   I had myself worried, too. (*Pulling out the handkerchief.*) But I had this.

**Elsa** (*taking the handkerchief back*)   I can't believe you held on to this tattered old thing.

**George**   Well, you told me to keep it safe. And thank you for sending me a message so wise it shamed this foolish knight. 'Hunt him where he lives.' Without this, we'd probably all still be lobbying some magistrate or other!

**Elsa**   George, I never sent any letter.

**Son** (*leading* **Henry**, *hands chained, into the crowd*)   Excuse me, sir, but that wasn't Elsa. It was Henry.

**Crier**   Henry?!

**Mrs Butcher**   Are you sure?

**Son**   I delivered the letter myself.

**Elsa**   You wrote to George?

**Henry**   A year ago, almost to the day, my freedom was taken from me. And it was no less than I deserved. But to see yours taken from you, to see you cast into a prison no less cruel, no less dark, when you'd done nothing at all to merit it . . .

**Elsa**   I'm so sorry, Henry, I had it all wrong –

**Henry**   I saw a chance to help and I took it, that's all.

**Miller**   Thank you, sir.

**Pike** (*to* **Son**)   Unchain him, son. (*To* **Henry**.) I want to shake his hand.

**Son** (*unchaining* **Henry**)   I told you he was all right, didn't I, Father?

**Pike**   You did, son. (*Helps with unchaining*.) Let's get these off you, lad.

**George**   Wait a moment. The Dragon's mark does not leave a man so easily.

**Henry**   Look: what do I have to do to convince you I've changed?

**Son** (*to* **George**)   He has, sir. He truly has.

**George**   Very well. Let him earn his place among us again. Little by little, day by day. (*To* **Henry**.) Let's see if you can serve this community as well as you once served your master.

**Henry**   Then I'll earn my place, sir. If that's what it takes.

*They finish unchaining* **Henry**.

**Brewer**   So what now?

**Mrs Butcher**   Well, we've made a bit of a mess, haven't we?

**Smith**   We do just as George said: break it apart from within, get rid of it all.

**Pike**   Get it back to how it used to be.

**Miller**   Tear down that awful mill, for a start.

**Alice**   Take all the wretched coal and burn it!

**Amy**   It's coal, Alice, that's what it's for.

**Ann**   Well, close the mines, in any case.

**Healer**   Let the night be the night and the day be the day.

**Healer's Daughter**   Live the way we used to.

**Crier**   Nice and small.

**George**   Sorry, stop: that isn't what I meant at all.

**Smith**   You what, sir?

**George**   That we should go back, that's not what I . . . Think of all that we've achieved here: the whole world looks to us now! Our inventions, our institutions. We can't tear *all* of it down!

**Pike**   But it just made us miserable, sir.

**George**   The Dragon made you miserable, Pike. But he's gone. And we're stronger and wiser and better now than ever before. (*Taking* **Elsa***'s hand.*) Our happiness is yet to come, I'm sure of it.

*A bright, high, piercing trumpet sounds.*

**Elsa**   The Brotherhood!.

**Boy**   The dragons are back!

**Charles**   George, be careful: there will be many battles to fight, and horrors unimaginable ahead.

**George**   I know, Charles, but I can no more refuse my duty than you can refuse yours.

**Elsa** (*taking out the handkerchief*)   I suppose you'll be wanting this back, then.

**George**   Elsa, I –

**Elsa**   Go. But I'm warning you, I'm expecting some serious courtship on your return. You owe me, sir.

**George**   It's a debt I'll be happy to pay. (*To everyone.*) And so it's goodbye to you all, once again. Keep this place safe until I return.

*He starts to go.*

**Boy**   Goodbye, George!

**Smith**   Good luck, sir!

**Crier**   Safe travels, Saint George!

*He's gone.*

**Brewer**   Well, let's get on with it, then.

**Healer**   Too right.

**Son**   But, it doesn't make sense: it's all this that's wrong, so how will making more of it make it right?

**Pike**   Come on, son. It's George. He's never steered us wrong before.

**Driver**   Well, he very nearly did.

**Mr Butcher**   But he's a knight.

**Mrs Butcher**   This is precisely my point: he's a knight, so we should do what he says.

*They start talking among themselves:*

**Driver**   Even if it doesn't make sense?

**Mrs Butcher**   Of course it makes sense: keep the good, throw out the bad, didn't you hear him?

**Driver**   I heard him right enough, madam.

**Mrs Butcher**   Oh, so you know better, do you? You know better than a knight: or do you have a plan of your own . . .

**Pike**   See, son, he's a knight. He knows what he's talking about.

**Son**   Look, I'm sure he means well, but it's not going to work.

**Pike**   Of course it is: we've just got to be different this time, in here.

**Son**   No I understood that bit, but it's all mixed together isn't it, the good and the bad . . .

**Henry** (*to everyone*)   Close your eyes.

**Elsa**   What?

**Henry**   Everyone, close your eyes. Shut them tight.

*They close their eyes.*

**Boy**   They're closed.

**Henry**   Now picture the future: imagine it's staring back at us. Right now. What do you see?

**Smith**   It's just dark.

**Henry**   No, come on, the future: what does it look like?

**Ann**   Well . . . we're warm.

**Healer's Daughter**   We're fed.

**Henry**   Yes?

**Healer**   Our children are safe.

**Henry**   Yes, good, keep going: what else do you see?

**Mrs Butcher**   There's food. Everywhere. Nobody goes to bed hungry.

**Healer's Daughter**   And nobody ever gets ill.

**Crier**   Vast new systems of communication.

**Driver**   The roads are smooth, and long.

**Amy**   And you can go anywhere, and do anything.

**Alice**   And everything's happening all at once.

**Smith**   We're flying!

**Pike**   Don't be soft, man.

**Smith**   Well maybe not literally flying.

**Miller**   No, we are, we're flying: higher and higher, and the air's getting warmer and the sky's getting brighter and we're flying, up and up and up towards the –

**Young Miller**   Sunshine.

*They all open their eyes.*

**Charles**   Well, it's not going to build itself now, is it?

*The townsfolk start to filter, slightly anxiously, out of the square.*

**Boy** (*going, to* **Elsa**)   And will we be happy there, Elsa?

**Elsa** (*going*) · What, boy?

**Boy** (*going*)   Will we be happy?

**Elsa** (*going*)   Yes, boy. We will. Oh, I hope that we will!

*And they're gone. The square is deserted. The* **Dragon***, dressed in a smart twenty-first-century suit, flies down from the sky and hovers over the land. He gazes out, smiling, into the solitary darkness. And then he roars.*

*Interval.*

# Act Three: City

## Chapter VIII
IN WHICH SAINT GEORGE RETURNS (AGAIN)

*Another year passes, and the town becomes a city: buildings increase in their stature and new ones jut up, massive turrets of glass pushing up into the air, and great grey edifices squatting on the landscape.*

*As the city folk work, and setting and costume evolve, they sing:*

**All** (*singing*)
Happy ever after now.
Build it brighter than the sun:
Build it free and build it proud,
And build it all for everyone.
We may have failed before but now we're wiser than we were,
So now's the time to seize the hour and build into the air:
Morning's glowing in the sky,
Hope is growing in our eyes,
Today
Is ours:
Let's get to work it's time to build it high!

Tear down the walls that hold us back,
Defeat the dragons of despair,
Slay the tyrants Loss and Lack,
Give everybody their fair share.
The road ahead is long but we'll walk it till we're through,
We'll keep moving on and on cos we've all got work to do.
Now morning's glowing in the sky,
And hope is growing in our eyes,
So hey,
Come on,
Let's get to work it's time to build it high!

In blocks of concrete, towers of glass,
Let's build a city safe and free,
Let's build our destiny at last,

Let's build our own prosperity.
Keep rolling on, my friends, the darkest hour is gone:
Through the night that never ends we can start to see the sun
And it's glowing in the sky
As hope is growing in our eyes,
So hey,
Come on,
Let's get to work it's time to build it high!

A beacon for the world with open arms and open doors,
Our happy-ever-after's ever closer than before:
Morning's glowing in the sky.
Hope is growing in our eyes,
So hey,
Come on,
Let's get to work it's time to build it high!

*The scene shifts to* **Charles** *and* **Elsa***'s cottage, which is now a twenty-first-century home. Though the layout remains the same as ever, the fixtures and fittings have modernised again: electric lights replace the gas lamps; the worryingly-groaning stove is gone, and in its place stands a kitchen worktop, with an oven built into it, and a microwave oven on top of it etc. Nothing here suggests chicness or wealth; rather a kind of cluttered and higgledy-piggledy normality.*

**Charles** *is in the kitchen. A smoke detector emits a loud piercing beeping sound. A plume of smoke emerges from the microwave behind him.*

**Charles**   Aah!!

*He rushes over to the microwave and opens its door, causing a vast billow of smoke to emanate from the microwave.*

No, no, no, no, no!

*He frantically begins to waft the smoke away.*

Aah! No, no, no, no, no!

*He grabs a tea-towel, pulls out a chair from the table, stands on the chair and begins energetically to waft the billowing smoke away from the smoke detector.*

No! No! No!

**George** *suddenly strides into the kitchen, still resplendent in his knightly armour but looking a little bedraggled and weary. He instantly sees the emergency and rushes to help* **Charles**. *They shout over the noise of the smoke detector.*

**George**   Charles!

**Charles**   George! You're back!

**George**   Yes!

**Charles** (*pointing*)   It's –

**George** *turns and sees where the smoke is coming from: the microwave. He dives towards it, and, with his gauntlet-protected hands, pulls out the smouldering, smoking bowl of chilli con carne. He holds the flaming bowl up to* **Charles**, *questioningly.*

**Charles** (*wafting smoke*)   Yes, put it down, George, put it down!

**George** *puts the flaming bowl down on the table.* **Charles** *is still wafting. They still shout.*

**Charles**   Now get the, the –

**George**   The –

**Charles**   The extinguisher!

**George**   The what?!

**Charles**   From under the sink!

**George**   Under the what?!

**Charles** (*pointing frantically*)   Over there! Under that! The red thing!

**George** *rushes to the sink, rummages in the cupboard underneath it, and emerges, holding a red hand-held fire extinguisher.*

**George**   This?!

**Charles**   Yes! Now press the button, press the –

**George** *presses the button on the extinguisher, which causes a powerful jet of foam to spurt into the air.* **George** *spins, gripping the spurting extinguisher, attempting to direct the foam towards the flaming bowl but initially hitting everything else in the process –* **Charles**, *the kitchen appliances, himself – before at last directing the spurt at the bowl for long enough to put out the fire.* **Charles** *continues wafting until the smoke detector stops a few moments later, and* **George** *and* **Charles** *stand, panting, both partially dowsed in foam, with the sodden chilli-covered, foam-drenched kitchen table between them, in silence.*

**Charles** (*panting*)    Welcome back, George.

**George** (*panting*)    It's good to be home. (*Looking at the extinguisher.*) This thing is extraordinary: a fire-squashing liquid!

**Charles** (*climbing down from the chair*)    I'm not sure I've got the hang of this oven. You see –

**George**    This strange tiny cube prepares your meals?

**Charles**    It does. Well, it's supposed to.

**George**    Extraordinary! Just look at this place! These orbs of light, this – What was this – (*Pointing at the sink.*) thing called again?

**Charles**    The sink.

**George**    This sink! What feats of craftsmanship, what marvels of imagination!

**Charles**    Yes, it is rather a lot.

**George**    Oh, don't be modest, Charles, I saw it all as I arrived: big red carriages, two storeys high and moving of themselves; pillars of glass, pushing up to the sky; people wandering around, entranced by little glowing screens, bumping into each other! I saw a sign for a musical revue about cats! About cats, Charles! I even saw a woman running, and I asked her where the danger was, and she said there wasn't a danger, and simply avowed that she liked running!

**Charles**   It is, George, but I sort of think I preferred it when it was all just a little bit simpler.

**George**   Really?

**Charles**   Well, you know where you are with a cast-iron pot and a fire, if you know what I mean.

**George**   Have no fear, Charles: I'm back, and I shall conquer this oven-cube –

**Charles**   Microwave.

**George**   I shall conquer this microwave, as I have conquered all the dragons in the world! Now, where's Elsa?

**Charles**   At work. She's a teacher now.

**George**   A teacher? How delightful, how apt! Beckoning the next generation over the horizon of adulthood; their little upturned faces, beaming gratefully. Do the lessons extend through the evening these days?

**Charles**   No, but it's a Friday so she's got the department meeting and then there's the gifted and talented club, but she'll be back any moment, I expect. I'd better get this cleaned up in the meantime. Could you give me a hand?

**George**   Certainly.

*He hands* **Charles** *a cloth.*

**Charles** (*looks at the cloth, then takes it*)   Oh, right then, I'll just –

*He starts cleaning.* **Elsa** *comes on, holding a pile of exercise books.*

**Elsa** (*not noticing* **George**)   I know I'm back late, I'm sorry, but I have a mountain of marking to do and I had to get on with some of it at school – (*She sees the state of the kitchen.*) Oh, Dad, what've you done? (*She goes over to the microwave.*) You can't put it in with the foil on!

**Charles**   No, I know.

**Elsa**   Well, you clearly don't because you've literally just tried to put it in with the foil on.

**Charles**   I thought you could.

**Elsa**   No, Dad, you can't – (*She sees* **George**.)

**George**   Hello!

**Elsa**   Hi.

**George**   I'm here! It's me.

**Charles**   It's George, Elsa! He's back!

**Elsa**   No, I can see that, Dad.

**George**   It's so good to see you Elsa, I'm so pleased to see you looking so well. (*Pulling out the handkerchief.*) Here's your handkerchief back, as promised, and I think I also owe you some, as you put it, 'serious courtship', so let's be about it, shall we? I saw somewhere called a 'Mega Bowl' on my way here and I thought it looked exciting: shall we go there?

**Elsa**   I –

**George**   Or there was a fish museum I passed as well, that looked fascinating.

**Elsa**   The fish museum? D'you mean the aquarium?

**George**   Or don't you like fish?

**Elsa**   I like fish just fine, it's just it's Friday night, George –

**George**   But I'm back, Elsa!

**Charles**   He's back, love!

**Elsa** (*to* **Charles**)   Dad, could you give us a minute, please?

**Charles**   Erm, yes, yes, of course, I'll just pop to the shop, see if they've got anything else for dinner. Is there anything you fancy? (*He catches her glare.*) No, I'll choose something myself, then.

*He bustles out.*

**George**   What's the matter, Elsa?

**Elsa**   I've got a lot of marking –

**George**    That can wait: what's wrong?

**Elsa**    I –

**George**    Aren't you pleased to see me?

**Elsa**    No I am, I really am, I'm thrilled.

**George**    Well you choose somewhere, then. Although, I have to say, the 'Mega Bowl' is still the most intriguing prospect as far as I'm concerned, I do want to see how big this bowl of theirs could possibly be, but no, you choose, you choose.

**Elsa**    What are you doing, George?

**George**    What?

**Elsa**    You can't just stroll back into my life and expect me to down tools and go to an aquarium!

**George**    Why not? It's what you said you wanted.

**Elsa**    I know, but –

**George**    Listen, I've been working all year, for –

**Elsa**    I've been working too.

**George**    Yes, but it's hardly the same, is it?

**Elsa**    Of course it's not the same, but it's not easy, if that's what you . . . Waking up when it's dark, flogging across the city to shout at a bunch of kids for a living, coming home, falling asleep in a pile of marking –

**George**    Well, you don't have to do that any more, because I'm back.

**Elsa**    I'm sorry? What do you mean I 'don't have to do that any more'? This is what I do, George, this is the life I've built for myself, you didn't expect me just to stand there, tied to a pole, waiting for you?

**George**    You don't believe me, do you?

**Elsa**    It's not that –

**George**   The dragons are dead, I've killed them all; and it was hard and muddy and one of them almost had me, but they're gone and it's done and I'm home.

**Elsa**   For how long, George?

**George**   For good.

**Elsa**   Sorry, but I've heard that before, look: I'm not stupid; that trumpet could sound any second and then you'd be straight off –

**George**   What do I have to do to convince you? Shall I take off my armour? Is that what you want?

**Elsa**   No –

**George**   I'll take off my armour.

*He starts taking off his armour.*

**Elsa**   Oh, don't be stupid.

**George**   No I'm taking it off! I'm taking off this. And this. And this. And this.

*He removes all of his armour.*

There! I've taken it off!

**Elsa**   That isn't the point, George.

**George**   So you still don't believe me?

**Elsa**   No, George, I –

**George**   All right, I'll throw it in the river, then, get rid of it for good! Would that make you happy?!

**Elsa**   Of course it won't make me happy.

**George**   At least you'll believe me then: at least you'll be convinced I'm done with it forever!

**Elsa**   If that's what you want to do –

**George**   It's not! It's not what I want to do, but if that's what you want me to do, then I'll do it!

**Elsa**   Fine.

**George**   Fine!

**Elsa**   Fine!

**George**   Fine: if you want me to throw it all in the river then that's exactly what I'll do. I'll take this sack – (*He picks up a laundry bag.*) and I'll do it!

**Elsa**   Go on then.

**George**   I will. And I might go and appraise the size of this 'Mega Bowl' while I'm at it.

**Elsa**   You do that, then: a bit of space might not be such a bad idea.

**George**   Goodbye, then.

**Elsa**   Bye.

*He leaves, with the bag. Silence.* **Charles** *returns, carrying a couple of cans of tinned food and a loaf of bread.*

**Charles**   Where's he off to with my laundry bag?

**Elsa**   He's throwing his armour in the river.

**Charles**   Right. I had quite a nice trip to the shop, actually. I found these tins of stew on one of the shelves in the corner, they look quite good. Nice and simple. I can't see a date on them anywhere but we should be okay.

**Elsa**   I'm not hungry, thanks, Dad.

**Charles** *goes to put the food down.*

**Charles**   I could hear you two bellowing at each other from half way up the street, you know.

**Elsa**   Right.

**Charles**   What are you doing, Elsa?

**Elsa**   I feel like he doesn't understand me, Dad.

**Charles**   I remember that lad the first time he turned up in this kitchen: scar dug deep in his chest, wound fresh as anything. And he stood right there where you're standing now, and he swore that no girl in the world could convince him to challenge the Dragon. And then you walked in, and, oh, my love, the look on his face . . . He's been running to catch up ever since. He loves you, my darling. Go after him.

**Elsa**   I don't –

**Charles**   Go on, off you go. And I'll get the dinner on in the meantime, and clean up the rest of this mess while I'm at it, with one of these blue fellows here.

**Elsa**   J-Cloth, Dad.

**Charles**   Right you are.

**Elsa** *sighs, smiles, goes over to her coat and puts it on.*


## Chapter IX
IN WHICH PATHS CROSS

*The city at night. A supermarket car park. A bench, next to a large clothes-recycling bank. The* **Boy** *and* **Young Miller** *are sitting on the bench. The* **Boy** *is dressed in a white football shirt, and has a large Saint George's cross painted on his face. He is playing a game on a hand-held games console.* **Young Miller** *is dressed in the uniform of a trainee supermarket baker – long white coat, mock old-fashioned apron, hair net etc. Silence.*

**Young Miller**   I'm waiting for my mum.

**Boy** (*playing the game*)   Right.

*Silence.*

**Young Miller**   She's picking me up, you see.

**Boy** (*playing the game*)   That's nice.

**Young Miller**   I work here now.

**Boy** (*playing the game*)   In the supermarket? Really?

**Young Miller**   Yes, I ice the iced buns, I drew spiders on the biscuits for Halloween.

**Boy** (*playing the game*)   Cool.

**Young Miller**   And they're going to teach me to do a tiger loaf eventually.

**Boy** (*playing the game*)   You like it, then?

**Young Miller**   It's fun. There was a fire alarm and we all stood in the rain, and once I found a pound left in a trolley, but I decided not to keep it, because the trolley belongs to –

**Boy** (*playing the game*)   Sorry, d'you mind, mate? I'm trying to play my game here.

**Young Miller**   What game is it?

**Boy** (*playing the game*)   You're like a knight, and there's different weapons, and different levels, and you have to kill all these dragons and stuff, it's –

**Young Miller**   What? (*Shaking.*) D . . . D . . .

**Boy** (*looking up*)   No, no, it's fine, mate, it's just a game.

**Miller**, *a department-store worker, arrives, flustered.*

**Miller**   Ooh, sorry I'm late, love, they're digging up the roundabout so the traffic's all on diversion. (*Sees him shaking.*) What's the matter?

**Young Miller** (*pointing at the* **Boy**)   He's got a . . . He's got a d . . . dra . . .

**Miller** (*to the* **Boy**)   What've you done to him?

**Boy**   I haven't done anything: he just asked about my game and I told him it had dragons in it and he started going all weird.

**Young Miller** (*reacting again to the* **Boy**'s *use of the word*) Dra . . . Dra . . .

**Miller** (*soothing*)   It's okay, son, shhh, it's okay. It's just a game.

**Young Miller**   But the drag . . .

**Miller** (*soothing, hugging* **Young Miller**)   Come on, now, son, shhh. (*To the* **Boy**.) Thanks a lot for that: d'you have any idea how hard he's been trying this year? He's been in groups, speech therapy, all sorts, he's been doing so well, and then you come along with your stupid game and set him off again!

**Boy**   But I –

**Young Miller**   I saw him. He was there.

**Miller**   You didn't see him, son: it's just a game, just a silly game played by a silly insensitive little boy.

**Young Miller**   D, d, d, d, d –

**Miller** (*to* **Young Miller**)   Do you know what I fancy? I really fancy a milkshake. Do you really fancy a milkshake too?

**Young Miller**   Yeah.

**Miller**   Shall we go to that diner on the way home, then, and get a milkshake? Would you like that?

**Young Miller**   Yeah, they've got new bubble-gum flavour, it's bright blue and tastes of actual bubble gum.

**Miller**   Well that sounds just delicious. Let's try that one, then, shall we?

**Young Miller**   Yeah.

**Miller** (*helping him up*)   Let's be having you, then, that's it. (*To the* **Boy**.) And I'd thank you not to terrify my son, in future.

*They leave.*

**Boy** (*going back to his game*)   No, no, no, come on!

**George**, *shorn of his armour, enters, and stands behind the* **Boy**, *watching him play.*

**Boy**   No, come on, die, die, die, come on!

**George**    Try the lance.

**Boy** (*he uses the lance and wins the game*)    Yes! Thanks mate – (*He turns and sees* **George**.) George!

*The* **Boy** *hugs* **George** *tight.*

**George**    Boy! I like your face.

**Boy**    What? Oh, yeah, this. It's for the match.

**George**    The what?

**Boy**    Did you kill all the dragons, then?

**George**    Yes, the dragon hunt is well and truly over. Except in that game of yours, it seems.

**Boy**    Is that why you don't have any armour on?

**George**    No, that was – Well, that was Elsa, actually.

**Boy**    She made you get rid of it?

**George**    No, I was the one who suggested it, but I feel like she wanted me to suggest it, you know, or she wanted me to want to suggest it, or something, I don't know.

**Boy**    Yeah, girls can be weird sometimes.

**George**    Indeed. I have to say, boy, I found the situation far more straightforward when she was tied to a stake or hitched to the gallows, clamouring to be rescued.

**Boy**    Well, maybe she doesn't want to be rescued any more.

**George**    Oh. Yes, you may have a point there. So what should I do now? I want to go back and apologise to her but she told me to give her some 'space', and I have frankly no idea what that means.

**Boy**    It means 'go away'.

**George**    Oh. Right, well, I suppose I'll just wander around for a while, then. The fish museum I had my eye on appears to be closed, and the 'Mega Bowl' turned out to be frankly a misnomer, but I've seen these big twirling sticks of meat about the place, so thought I might try one of those.

**Boy**   Ugh, no way mate: we're going to the pub.

**George**   What?

**Boy**   Well, you need cheering up, and I want to watch the match. Look, I got all dressed up and saved up all my pocket money for drinks, but they won't let me in without a responsible adult, so that's going to be you.

**George**   I'm really not sure I'm ready for a homecoming just yet, boy: I feel a little out of sorts tonight.

**Boy**   I know: you can go in disguise! Then no one will know it's you, and you won't have to talk to people if you don't want to. Please. It's the quarter final, George.

**George**   I don't have any other garments.

**Boy**   We can look in here. I got these – (*His shorts.*) from it. It's basically free clothes. (*He goes to the clothing bank.*) Come on, give me a hand.

**George** *helps the* **Boy** *look through the clothing bank.*

**Boy** (*pulling out clothes*)   Here we go. Put these on.

**George** (*putting on the clothes*)   Yes, I ought to pass quite incognito as I summon a flagon of ale.

**Boy**   Order a pint, you mean.

**George**   'Order a pint.' Is that what they're saying these days?

**Boy**   Yeah, we might need to work on that.

**George**   How do I look?

**Boy**   Erm. Awesome.

**George** *looks ridiculous.*

**George**   Really?

**Boy**   You'll need a new name, too.

**George**   A name?

**Boy**   Well I can't call you George, can I?

**George**   How about . . . 'Lancelot'?

**Boy**   I was thinking more like 'Ian'.

**George**   'Ian Lancelot': I like it!

**Boy**   No. Just Ian.

**George**   Very well.

**Boy**   Come on then, Ian.

*Silence.*

That's you.

**George**   Ah, yes.

**Boy**   Let's go.

*Meanwhile, in another part of the city,* **Henry**, *in full community service apparel (overalls, high-vis tabard, electronic ankle tag etc.), is picking up litter using a metal claw-tool and putting it into a large bin-bag. There are several full bin-bags just behind him. He looks extremely beleaguered by the work.* **Elsa** *arrives, searching for* **George**. *She sees* **Henry** *and stops, then attempts to sneak past him without being noticed.* **Henry** *turns and sees her, and calls out.*

**Henry**   Elsa!

**Elsa** *ignores him and keeps going.*

**Henry**   Elsa! Wait! Elsa!

**Elsa** (*turning back, embarrassed, pretending she hadn't heard him*) Oh, Henry. Hi. Sorry. What's up?

**Henry**   Oh, nothing, I, sorry, I, well I just wanted to say hi, like, I just saw you there and, well, I haven't seen you in ages, how are you doing –

**Elsa**   Henry, I –

**Henry**   In fact, I was thinking of you the other day, actually, I was scrubbing some of the graffiti off the underpass someone had written in big letters 'I never finish anyth –', and like they hadn't actually finished the word, and I thought you'd love that –

**Elsa**   Henry –

**Henry**   You see, because they haven't actually finished the word, that's the joke, they never finish anyth –

**Elsa**   I'm really sorry, I'm in a bit of a hurry and, sorry, I've got to –

*The three* **Fielder Sisters** *rush on. They're dressed for a hen night (pink sashes, fake tiaras etc.), and are very drunk, especially* **Ann**.

**Alice**   Where are we?

**Amy**   We're in the city!

**Ann**   We're in heaven!

**Alice** (*shouting at* **Henry**)   Hey, mate, where are we?!

**Ann**   Where are we, mate?

**Amy** (*going over to* **Henry**)   Henry, is there a club nearby?

**Alice** (*also approaching* **Henry**)   Henry, Henry, is there a club? All the pubs are rammed cos of the football.

**Henry**   I'm probably not the best person to –

**Amy**   We need a club, Henry!

**Ann** (*also approaching* **Henry**, *putting her arm around* **Amy**)   My sister's getting married, you see!

**Alice**   Shh, it's a secret!

**Amy**   I'm getting married!

**Ann**   And even though she's younger than me I'm not bothered at all!

**Henry**   I think there's –

**Alice**   Amy, look: it actually says 'Community Service' on the back of his –

**Amy**   Community service!

**Ann** (*mock official*)   For your service to the community, sir: we salute you! (*Salutes.*)

**Alice**   Oh look, he's got a tag and all.

**Amy**   Give us a look at your tag? Come on, let's see it!

**Henry** (*showing them his ankle tag*)   It doesn't come off, I'm afraid.

**Ann** (*getting way too close to* **Henry**)   Ooh, ankle, very cute, very sexy! Extremely –

**Amy**   Okay, let's go, Ann.

**Ann**   Maybe you could marry me, Henry –

**Henry**   No, I don't –

**Amy**   Come on, Ann!

**Ann**   No, let's get married, don't be shy, let's get married, come on!

*She grabs* **Henry**'s *arm and marches him around.*

**Alice**   Ann, let's go, come on!

**Amy**   Come on, Ann!

**Ann**   I tried to marry this guy in the chippie but he jilted me! I was jilted, Henry! So come on, let's do this!

**Alice**   Come on, Ann.

**Ann** *grabs one of the rubbish bags, tears it open and throws the contents into the air.*

**Ann**   Confetti! Confetti!

**Alice**   Ann!

**Ann** *tears open another bag and throws that everywhere too.*

**Ann**   Confetti! Photos! Reception!

**Amy** (*grabbing her and starting to march her off*)   Let's go, Ann.

**Ann**   Honeymoon! House! Baby! Happiness!

**Alice** (*marching her off*)   All right, Ann. (*To* **Henry**.) Sorry, Henry.

**Ann**   Have a good night!

*They go.* **Henry** *and* **Elsa** *stand amid the strewn rubbish.* **Henry** *sighs.*

**Elsa**   Does that happen a lot?

**Henry**   Weirdly, more often than you'd think.

*He starts picking up the rubbish.*

**Elsa**   Listen, Henry, I never got to say to you: thank you. For what you did last year. That letter. And I was just awful to you, but if it wasn't for you'd we'd all be –

**Henry**   Don't worry about it.

**Elsa**   Well anyway, I'm glad you're . . . I was going to say 'free' but I guess that's not technically true.

**Henry**   No, it's cool: community service isn't too bad. It's kind of meditative. And you get breaks like in a normal job, and, well, I suppose there's quite a large element of being spat on, but it's better than that tiny cell, at least. (*Sees* **Elsa** *picking up the rubbish too.*) You don't have to do that.

**Elsa**   Seriously, it's fine. I don't know where I'm going anyway.

*He watches her.*

**Henry**   Are you all right?

**Elsa**   Yeah. It's just, well, George is back and we had a massive fight, of course, as soon as he got here, and now I can't find him.

**Henry**   He's back?

**Elsa**   Yep.

**Henry**   Well that's great. That's totally great for you.

**Elsa**    I know, but it's all very complicated, and I'm thrilled, of course I am, but I said something stupid and then he went off to throw his armour in the river.

**Henry**    Why did he do that?

**Elsa**    To prove he's given it all up for good. But now I don't know where he is.

**Henry**    He'll be back.

**Elsa**    He might not be. I truly was a massive dick to him.

**Henry**    I'm sure you weren't.

*They pick up the rubbish, in silence.*

**Elsa**    It's just, it wasn't what I expected, you know? You dream about this moment, you make, like, a plan in your head, you map it all out, you have a list of everything you'd say, and then he's just there, and it doesn't come out.

*They pick up the rubbish.*

**Henry**    Like what?

**Elsa**    What?

**Henry**    Like what? What would you say?

*Silence.*

**Elsa**    Like . . . I guess I'd just say . . . hello. I guess I'd just say . . . I missed you. I guess I'd just say I'm doing all right. I'd say I'm a terrible cook. I'd say I like watching the telly. I'd say there are good days and bad. I'd say I've started doing yoga. I read about stuff. I want to be good. Like one day a few months ago I thought I'd sell my computer and give loads of clothes to the charity shop and eat only stuff from the fair-trade place on the corner and I stopped driving the car but I lasted like eight days then I realised I couldn't just do *those* things I'd have to stop paying taxes and burn all my money and quit my job and I actually quite like my job even though kids can be completely demonic even though I get home in the evenings and sometimes just inexplicably cry at the weather forecast or for no real reason at all which I've been doing a lot recently actually on buses as well and sometimes I think I see other people inexplicably crying as well but instead of looking at each other and seeing if we're okay we just turn away and look back out the window or whatever and I know it sounds like I've gone a bit off-topic here but these are really all the things I want to say, and so I'd say them. And then I'd stop. And then he'd hug me. And he'd understand. And that would be . . . so nice.

**Henry**   Go and say that, then.

**Elsa**   Right, yeah. Yeah.

**Henry**   I mean, how much time have you actually spent with each other? You've got to forgive him if he doesn't actually know you that well.

**Elsa**   He wanted to go to the Mega Bowl.

**Henry**   Wow.

**Elsa**   I went but he wasn't there.

**Henry**   I mean, can you imagine him?

**Elsa**   Don't.

**Henry**   Renting those red and white shoe things? He'd probably start jousting the pins.

**Elsa** (*laughing*)   Yeah.

**Henry**   Listen, Elsa, I do want to say, if you ever –

**Elsa**   It's just I love him, Henry. He's all I ever think about.

*Silence.*

**Henry**   Try the pub.

**Elsa**   What?

**Henry**   Try the pub. I saw a guy who looked a bit like him headed that way wearing the most ridiculous outfit I've ever seen so it was either George or some kind of homeless clown. So that's where he'll be, I reckon.

**Ann** *runs through again, with a traffic cone on her head.*

**Ann**    I'm the traffic wizard! Woooo!

**Elsa** (*to* **Henry**)    At least someone's having a good night. Thanks, Henry.


## Chapter X
IN WHICH THERE'S A KNIGHT IN THE PUB

*The pub.* **Crier**, **Smith**, **Driver**, **Son**, **Healer**, **George** *and the* **Boy** *are watching the match.* **Brewer**, *behind the bar, is also watching.* **Healer's Daughter** *is collecting glasses and wiping down tables, watching intermittently. Everyone, excluding the staff and the* **Boy**, *but including, particularly,* **George**, *has been drinking. A massive celebration: the island's team have scored!*

**Crier**    Yes!

**Brewer**    Get in!

**Healer**    One–nil!

*The city folk continue cheering:* **George**, *in the centre, hugs the* **Boy**, *high-fives* **Driver**, *chest-bumps* **Smith** *and* **Son** *in quick succession, then performs a short medieval dance.*

**Crier** (*about* **George**)    Look at him go!

**All** (*as* **George** *dances*)    I–an, I–an, I–an, I–an, I–an, I–an –

**George** *ends on a pose, and the city folk cheer.*

**George** (*grabbing his pint and mounting a stool*)    My friends: a toast! To this mighty game we call 'Foot Ball'; and to victory!

**All**    To victory!

**George** *downs his pint to the continued chant of 'I–an, I–an, I–an', and then smashes his empty glass down on to the floor.*

**George**   Another drink! Drinks for everyone!

**Crier** (*watching the match*)   Shh, shh, shh, they're starting again: their ball.

**Smith** (*watching the match*)   We can't throw this lead away, lads, come on!

**Brewer**   What you having, then, Ian?

**George**   Well I'll have four of those upside-down bottles, please, six of the big red ones, one of those, what's that?

**Brewer**   Tequila.

**George**   Yes, one of those, and five of every beer.

**Boy** (*to* **George**, *nudging him*)   But we don't have any money.

**George** (*to* **Brewer**)   Just wait a moment, please, mate.

**Driver** (*watching the match*)   Wow, they're annoyingly good, aren't they?

**Crier** (*watching the match*)   But, oh, look at that: two of our boys, closed it right down!

**George** (*to the* **Boy**)   How much do we have?

**Boy** (*counting*)   Five twenty-one.

**George** (*to* **Brewer**)   And how much will five twenty-one get us?

**Brewer**   A pint and a packet of peanuts.

**George**   A pint and a packet of peanuts, please, mate!

**Crier** (*watching the match*)   Lovely little through-ball from the captain, into the centre.

**Son** (*watching the match*)   He's running clear. (*Clapping.*) Come on, keep pushing!

**Driver** (*watching the match*)   Edge of the area: shoot, shoot!

**George** (*watching the match*)   Kick the ball into the rectangle with your foot!

**Smith**   You what?

**Boy**   This is his first ever match, isn't it, Ian?

**Brewer** (*bringing* **George** *his drink*)   You've never seen a football match before?

**George**   Well, no, I've been –

**Boy**   He was raised in the woods, you see.

**George**   Yes, yes, I was.

**Driver**   What, by wolves?

**George**   Yes!

**Boy**   No!

**George**   No!

**Boy**   So he didn't have a telly, did you, Ian?

**George**   Out of respect for the wolves.

**Healer** (*to the* **Boy**)   How do you know him, then?

**Boy**   We met at the . . . zoo.

**George**   I'm a zookeeper.

**Smith**   Oh, wow.

**George**   Yes, I keep a little zoo. (*Goes into his pocket and mimes pulling out something small.*) Here it is. A nice little zoo. This is what I keep. Shhh, the animals are sleeping.

**Crier** (*watching the match*)   Ooh, opposition's charging forward now.

**Smith** (*watching the match*)   We've gotta watch out for that striker of theirs, he's a machine.

**Driver** (*watching the match*)   Takes a little shot –

**Son** (*watching the match, clapping*)   Lovely save: get in!

**Smith** (*chanting*)   You will ne–ever, you will ne–ever –

**All** (*chanting*)   You will ne–ever score a goal! You will ne–ever score a goal!

**George**   What's this?

**Boy**   It's a chant.

**George**   And what's a chant?

**Boy**   It's when you do a little song, to insult the other team.

**Crier** (*chanting*)   Too slow, and you know you are!

**All** (*chanting*)   Too slow, and you know you are, too slow, and you know you are! Too slow, and you know you are!

**George** (*to the tune of 'Greensleeves'*)
     Ye blockish knaves you cannot play:
     You've shamed even your worthless land;
     Disgraced your mothers and smirched your name,
     You're a low band of ignorant horse-thieves!

*Silence. Then everyone breaks into cheers and laughter.*

**Son**   You're a legend, Ian!

**Smith**   Legend!

**George**   Yes, I am a legend: I am a legend!

**Crier** (*back to the football*)   Nice little clearance there.

**Driver** (*watching*)   Yes!

**George**   Oh, this is just marvellous, isn't it?

**Smith**   I've said it before: this might just be our year.

**George**   Might be? It is! That trophy is as good as ours, Smith, I can feel it!

**Brewer**   Steady on there, Ian.

**George**   Oh, 'steady on' be damned: we're going to win!

**Brewer**   I appreciate you're new to this, Ian, but it doesn't really work like that.

**George**    What d'you mean?

**Brewer**    Well, basically every time there's a tournament we all get together in the pub, and we shout at the telly, get drunk and break our usual custom of not talking to strangers to turn to each other and say 'this is our year', and then we pin all our hopes on a bunch of overpaid teenagers, reminisce about that one time ages ago when we won, and then we inevitably mess it all up and get booted out early so we cry a bit and say we're not crying, come up with some theories about the failure of our defensive formation, get a bit more drunk, kick over a bin and the next day the manager gets sacked and we get a new manager and do it all over again, in an endless cycle of hope and despair that's sort of our national pastime.

**George**    Right.

**Brewer**    So I wouldn't get your hopes up, is all I'm saying.

**George**    Oh nonsense, sir: I may have been abroad fighting –

**Boy**    In the woods –

**George**    I may have been in the woods fighting zoos, but I know this land to be the home of champions, and victory is not simply something we deserve, it is our birthright, mate!

*The match-watchers let out a unified groan.*

**George**    What? What happened?

**Crier**    They've equalised.

**Son**    One all.

**Brewer** (*going back to the bar*)    Told you.

**George**    So what happens now?

**Boy**    We've got to score another goal.

**Driver**    See, they capitalise, they get in there. That's what we need to do.

**Smith**    Right, don't worry, everyone: our lads have got this, I know it.

**George**   Of course they have, they're the lads!

**Son**   How do you 'know it', Smith?

**Smith**   I can see it, can't I? In their eyes: they've got the look.

**Driver**   What look? The look of a bunch of illiterate, wife-beating prima donnas?

**Smith**   No: the look that wins wars, that builds railways and canals and big long roads and massive bridges and the finest healthcare system known to man, that basically invents pop music, and the computer, or the internet, or both –

**Son**   Oh, what are you on about, Smith, man? You ought to read a book every once in a while.

**Smith**   I do read, I –

**Son**   I'm not talking about big pop-up ones with pictures. You think we deserve to win just because we did some good stuff in the past? What about when we enslaved whole peoples, committed mass genocides, drew borders everywhere till the whole world was at war, pillaged and looted and grew rich and fat off the suffering of others. Or are we not talking about that?

**Smith**   I –

**Son**   I'm going for a slash.

*He goes.*

**Smith** (*calling after him*)   I, I do read, you know! (*To everyone.*) I'm on a novel a week for the wife's book group!

**George**   What was all that about?

**Smith**   He's an uppity little pillock, that's what. Ever since he started that degree of his. Well, the joke'll be on him in two years' time, when he's up to his eyeballs in debt, with no prospects.

**Driver**   Oh, leave him, Smith, he's all right.

**Smith**  No, he's a pillock. If it weren't for the fact that I'm mates with his dad, I'd have knocked his smug little –

**Healer**  Smith.

**Smith** (*to* **George**)  Sorry. I shouldn't have – Don't tell him I said that, will you?

**Crier** (*watching the match*)  Oh, we need to get it out to the wings, come on.

**Driver** (*watching the match*)  We can't hack the pressure, can we? We're falling apart.

**George**  Oh nonsense, madam: look at what they're wearing on their breast.

**Driver**  The cross?

**George**  The cross, exactly, madam. Each and every one of them a knight!

**Driver**  You ought to get out more, Ian, mate.

**George**  What did you say?

**Driver** (*topping up her drink with her hip-flask*)  I used to drive long-haul, Ian, so I've been about a bit, and I can tell you this for free: that cross doesn't mean what you think it does.

**George**  That's where you're wrong –

**Driver**  Sorry to burst your bubble, mate, but we're the only ones flying that flag these days, though most of us are too embarrassed to actually fly it. We're not a nation of knights, my friend: we're a nation of has-beens, the lot of us. (*Raising her glass.*) Cheers.

*The **Fielder Sisters** come in.*

**Alice**  Oh, is the match still going? What's the score?

**Crier**  One all.

**Smith**  They've been faffing about in midfield for ages.

**Brewer** (*to the* **Fielders**)   I thought you'd left this place off your pub crawl.

**Amy**   Yeah, we did. But they wouldn't let us into the Honey Shack because *somebody* kept trying to marry the bouncer.

**Ann**   Let's just get a drink.

**Alice** (*pointing at* **George**)   Who's this?

**George**   Miss, I am Saint –

**Boy**   Ian! It's Ian!

**Brewer**   He's new.

**George** (*bowing*)   Ladies.

**Crier** (*watching the match*)   Their defence is far too tight, it's like a brick wall.

**Driver** (*watching the match*)   They're marking our lads too hard.

**Crier** (*watching the match*)   Send it back, then, boys, make a bit of space!

**Healer** (*watching the match*)   Go on, lads!

**George** (*watching the match*)   Go on!

**Smith** (*watching the match*)   Come on: it's time for a bit of magic!

**George**   Let's have some magic, then!

*He launches into his dance and everyone whoops and cheers.* **Ann** *begins dancing with* **George**.

**Ann**   You don't fancy getting married, do you?

**Alice** (*pulling* **Ann** *away*)   No, Ann.

**Amy** (*pulling* **Ann** *away*)   Let's go.

**George** (*stops dancing, dizzy*)   Ooh, I'm – Everything's gone a bit shaky.

**Smith**   You all right, Ian?

**George**    Yes, I'm – You wouldn't happen to know where the privy is, would you?

**Smith** (*pointing*)    Just through there.

**George** *stumbles out. Pike's* **Son** *sits back down.*

**Son**    How long's left?

**Crier** (*watching the match*)    Three minutes. This is it now: we really need to start creating chances.

**Smith** (*watching the match*)    Come on, break through, break through.

*The match-watchers groan.*

This is a joke.

**Son**    I thought they had it all under control, Smith. I thought they had 'the look'.

**Smith**    Shut up, lad.

**Son**    We're just gonna do what we do every time: lose our nerve in the last couple of minutes. Fall apart at the back. And then they'll be straight in like a pack of dogs and we'll be done.

**George** *emerges from the toilet, practically mummified with toilet paper.*

**George**    I honestly don't know what happened.

**Healer's Daughter** (*starting to unwrap* **George**)    Stand still a sec.

**Crier** (*watching the match*)    Come on, just get in space, get in space!

**Healer** (*watching the match*)    Get in space, lads! Come on!

**Healer's Daughter** (*rolling her eyes*)    Ugh.

**George**    What's the matter?

**Healer's Daughter**    It's just my mum. Pretending she likes football cos she doesn't have any friends. She just doesn't –

**George** (*spitting out toilet paper*)   It's gone in my mouth.

**Healer's Daughter**   I'm sorry, it's just . . . she's doing my head in at the moment. She's constantly on at me for dropping out of medical school, for not getting my own place.

**Smith** (*watching the match*)   Oh, ref, that was never a foul, he dived!

**Healer** (*watching the match*)   Looks like they're bringing on the stretcher.

**Smith** (*watching the match*)   Oh. Maybe it was a foul, then.

**George**   You ought to tell her to desist.

**Healer's Daughter**   No, it's fine. I'm getting out of here anyway.

**George**   You're leaving?

**Healer's Daughter**   Yep: a bus then a train then a plane.

**George**   Why would you want to leave?

**Healer's Daughter**   I hate it here.

**George**   But these tables, these little wet mat things –

**Healer's Daughter** ( *finishes unwrapping* **George**)   Look, I shouldn't have said that, I haven't told her yet. You won't say anything, will you?

**George**   I give you my word, miss. Now, I'm going to need another glass of pints.

**George** *stumbles over to the bar.*

**Crier** (*watching the match*)   Right, they're off again.

**Smith** (*watching the match*)   How long will they add?

**Crier** (*watching the match*)   Dunno: two minutes, three minutes max.

**George** (*to the* **Boy**)   Can I have more pints, please?

**Boy**   I've run out of money.

**Healer**    I'll get you one, Ian. (*To* **Brewer**.) Whatever he's drinking.

**George**    Thank you, madam.

**Healer**    Life and soul of the party, isn't she?

**George**    Who?

**Healer**    My daughter. Sorry you had to be on the receiving end of that: I hope she didn't ruin your night with her moaning.

**Brewer** (*giving* **George** *the pint*)    There you are.

**Healer**    I wouldn't take it personally, Ian. She's like that with everything, has been for ages.

**George**    You ought to tell her to desist.

**Healer**    Well, I would, but she barely talks to me. She blocked me from her phone the other day. It's just childish, really.

**Smith** (*watching the match*)    No, get in there!

**Crier** (*watching the match*)    Close it down!

**Healer**    Oh, I shouldn't have said that. You won't say anything, will you?

**George**    Of course not.

**Son** (*watching the match*)    This is a disaster waiting to happen. A total disaster.

**George**    What? Why has all the winning stopped?

**Son**    There's no way we can win if it goes to penalties, Ian. We're completely awful at penalties.

**George**    Have faith, my friends! It isn't over yet!

**Boy**    It nearly is.

**Brewer**    See, Ian: what did I say?

**Son**    This is just what we always do.

**Alice**  We're rubbish!

**Ann**  Terrible!

**George**  No, no, don't say that: we have to keep our spirits up, come on!

*He dances.*

Come on! I–an, I–an, I–an!

**Crier**  Leave it, Ian.

**Son**  Ian, this is important now.

**Driver**  Joke's over, Ian.

**George**  Come on! (*Singing.*) Ye blockish knaves you cannot play –

**Smith**  Shut up, mate!

**Son**  Seriously!

**Boy**  Please –

**George**  No, I will not stand for this, I will not! Where's the – give me the –

*He grabs the remote and stands on a chair. He turns off the television.*

There.

**Crier**  Ian!

**George**  No! They can hear you! Those lads! As you heap your reckless calumny upon them! 'Rubbish!' 'Awful!'

**Boy**  No they can't.

**George**  Can they not?

**Boy**  No, it's a telly, Ian.

**George**  They can still hear you, though: in their hearts!

*Everyone is trying to grab the remote from* **George**.

**Smith**  Ian!

**Crier**   Ian!

**George**   Do you have any idea how hard it is? To wear that cross? To bear the hopes and dreams of a nation on your shoulders? You go out there and you put your blood and body on the line and then you come home and she's not even pleased to see you, and she's just mean –

**Smith**   Ian, just leave it, will you?

**George**   I will not: you owe them!

**Healer**   Come on, Ian!

**George**   You owe them your faith! You owe them your support! They cannot fight without it! They're only losing because you're willing them to lose! So just stop it, stop it at once, and get behind them. We're the greatest nation on the face of the Earth and we are going to win!

*Pike's **Son** manages to grab the remote and turns the television back on.*

**Driver**   What's that? What's happening?

**Healer**   They're celebrating.

**Son**   What? What about?

**Boy**   Why are they cheering?

**Crier**   They've scored. They've scored!

**Brewer**   They've gone ahead!

**Alice**   No!

**Smith**   No, no, there's still the . . . there's still the – (*Hearing it.*) final whistle.

*Silence. Everyone slowly turns and glares at **George**.*

**George**   Well, to be perfectly frank, I'm not surprised.

**Brewer**   You'd better watch it, pal.

**George**   I'm not surprised! When I see the way you – (*To **Brewer**.) take pride in your failure – (*To **Son**.) spit on your history – (*To* **Driver**.) slander your own reputation, is it any wonder you don't have it in you to wallop a bunch of horse thieves at the foot ball?! You're pathetic, all of you! Pathetic!

**Healer**   Steady on, Ian.

**George**   I'm sorry, are you telling me to steady on, madam? You who have been such a harridan to your daughter that you've driven her out of her home?! She's leaving, madam, and all because of you!

**Healer** (*to* **Daughter**)   What?!

**George**   I should imagine it's a relief, is it not? (*To* **Daughter**.) She thinks you're a whining little child! So don't you tell me –

**Healer's Daughter** *starts to storm off.*

**Healer** (*going after her*)   You come back here now!

**Son**   Look, mate: you just can't do that.

**George**   Don't you tell me what to do: nobody here even likes you!

**Son**   What? That's not true –

**George** (*pointing at* **Smith**)   He hates you! He wants to knock your block off!

**Smith**   I didn't say that, I –

**George**   An uppity little pillock, is that what you called him?

**Son** (*to* **Smith**)   Right. You. We're having words.

**Brewer**   Ian, I'm going to have to ask you to leave.

**George**   No, no, I will not: how dare you, how dare you?!

**Crier**   It's over, mate.

**George** (*to* **Brewer**)   Don't you tell me what to do! I'm a trained warrior –

**Brewer**   Right, that's it.

**George** (*to* **Brewer**)  Get off me, sir: your beer tastes like the urine of an elderly mule! (*To* **Ann**.) Miss, I wouldn't marry you for the largest dowry in the kingdom! (*To* **Driver**.) And as for you, madam: you have a drinking problem! And you're sour!

**Driver** *head-butts* **George**, *who gets attacked from several directions, but the* **Boy** *grabs him and begins to bundle him out. Meanwhile,* **Healer** *and* **Daughter** *are screaming at each other, and* **Smith** *and* **Son** *start to fight.* **Crier** *and* **Driver** *get pulled into the fight between* **Smith** *and* **Son**. *Drinks get spilled on the* **Fielder Sisters** *and they join the general mêlée.*


## Chapter XI
IN WHICH PATHS DIVERGE

*A row of public bins, with a sloped walkway curving above them. A homeless man sleeps down by the bins, off to the side. The* **Boy** *and* **George**, *just out of the pub, enter briskly.*

**Boy** (*leading* **George** *up the walkway*)  Come on, let's go, come on.

**George** (*following*)  But, wait, what –

**Boy**  Come on, quick!

**George**  But what on Earth just happened?!

**Boy**  It's how they always are, they're always shouting!

**George**  They're –

**Boy**  Getting angry and sad about the smallest things, I can't take it! And then saying sorry every five minutes even though they're not sorry at all. And blaming everything on someone else even though it's not their fault either, and going around all red in the face and ready to snap, and going outside and getting cross with other people for walking too fast or too slow, and going through all the TV channels too quick so I can't watch anything, and telling me not to talk on the bus, not to play in the fountain, not to sing in the zoo, and going on holiday cos they don't like it here and then getting annoyed cos there isn't the same stuff we have at home, and voting for things all the time, and not being happy ever, and popping to the shops every five minutes because they've forgotten stuff, and getting angry with themselves for being angry in the first place, cos even though things are supposed to be so much better now it really doesn't feel that way at all!

**George**   Heavens above!

**Boy**   And now we've lost the match it's gonna get even worse!

**George**   I honestly thought we were going to win, I honestly thought we'd won.

**Boy**   And now I feel all stupid with this on my face. I'm going home!

*The **Boy** stomps off, sad.*

**George**   But, boy –

*He turns and looks out over the city.*

(*Calling out.*) I know not what you've done or how you've done it, but you're out there, oh, you're out there: I can smell you in the air! Now show yourself, I dare you! Show yourself!

*A dog starts barking. People shout out from the neighbouring buildings.*

**Voice 1**   Give it a rest: we've got a baby up here!

**Voice 2**   Stop shouting, you!

**George** (*still calling out*)   I know you to be sly and full of cunning, I know that honour is beyond your breed, but you cannot refuse me. And so I bid you: show yourself! Dragon, I challenge you!

*A voice from the sleeping bag answers him:*

**Dragon** (*in gruff tones*)   Would you mind keeping it down, mate? Some of us are trying to get some sleep!

**George**   Oh, deepest apologies, sir, I –

*The* **Dragon** *crawls out of the sleeping bag and stands in the dim light.*

**Dragon**    Good evening, George.

**George**    You! I knew it!

*He drops down from the walkway. The* **Dragon** *raises his hat, and darts out.*

**George**    Wait! Come back here! Wait!

*He starts out after the* **Dragon**. **Elsa** *comes on, from the other side.*

**Elsa**    George!

**George** *(turning)*    Elsa! I –

**Elsa**    I'm sorry. I was an absolutely massive dick to you, I think I was just in shock or something, and – what on Earth are you wearing?

**George** *(looking off to where the* **Dragon** *went)*    Yes, look: no more armour.

**Elsa**    Listen: let's just go home. Dad's got the dinner on, I mean, I'm not actually sure what was in that tin of his, but –

**George** *(still looking off to where the* **Dragon** *went)*    Well, that sounds completely delicious, but there's just a thing I have to do first, there's something that's come up, an old friend.

**Elsa**    Right. Of course. That's totally cool. Sure. I'm just glad we're okay.

**George** *(running off)*    Yes, everything is excellent it's –

*He runs out, after the* **Dragon**. **Elsa** *looks slightly perplexed, but turns and walks out, in the opposite direction.*

## Chapter XII
IN WHICH THERE IS A DRAGON-HUNT

*The city at night.* **George** *rushes drunkenly through the dark streets, in search of the* **Dragon***. He spots the homeless man, and chases after him.*

**George**   Get back here! Stop!

**Miller** *and* **Young Miller** *arrive, on the other side of the street.*

**Miller**   Come on, son: we're nearly at the car.

**Young Miller**   It's too loud, Mum!

**Miller**   Just put your fingers in your ears, then.

**George** *grabs and turns the homeless man: it's not the* **Dragon***.*

**Homeless Man**   Oi, what you doing, mate? Get off me!

**George**   Sorry. I thought you were –

**Dragon** *(he has suddenly taken* **Young Miller***'s place, in the supermarket baker's uniform)*   Leave that poor man alone, George. I expected better of you.

**Miller** *heads out, with the* **Dragon***.* **George** *lurches after him. Meanwhile* **Crier** *and* **Healer** *have arrived, helping* **Smith***, who has been punched in the fight, and now has his head back, covered by an ice pack.*

**Healer**   Just keep the ice pack on, there you go.

**Crier**   It's all right, Smith, we're getting you home.

**Healer**   Just hold on.

**Dragon** *has suddenly taken* **Smith***'s place, removing the ice pack to reveal himself.*

**Dragon** *(to* **George***)*   I thought you wanted to challenge me, George? Well be about it then!

**George** *runs over to* **Smith***.*

**George**    Come here, monster! (*He grabs the ice pack and removes it.*) Show yourself!

**Smith** (*who is now back in his place*)    Ow! What you doing?

**Crier**    Get out of it! Go on! You've caused enough trouble for one night.

**Crier** *shoves* **George** *away.* **Crier**, **Healer** *and* **Smith** *head out.* **George** *stumbles, and looks around frantically. Meanwhile the* **Fielder Sisters** *arrive. They have now acquired a shopping trolley, in which* **Ann** *has passed out.* **Amy** *pushes the shopping trolley and* **Alice** *holds on to the front.*

**Alice** (*holding on to the trolley*)    Wooo!

**Ann**    Where are we?

**Amy**    We're getting a kebab!!

**Alice** (*laughing*)    You're going too fast, Amy. It's too fast!

**Amy**    But it's shutting soon!

**Alice**    I'm going to be sick . . .

*The trolley crashes. The* **Dragon** *leaps out, taking* **Alice**'s *place, in a hen-night outfit.*

**Dragon**    You'll have to do better than that!

*The* **Dragon** *laughs and appears to dart into a shut-up shop. The* **Fielder Sisters** *head out.*

**George**    Get back here, beast!

*He runs to the shop and starts hammering on the shutters, kicking and punching them, shouting as he does so:*

Come out and fight me, come on! Show yourself! Show yourself!

**Mrs Butcher** *arrives, in her dressing gown, from the house next door.*

**Mrs Butcher**    What on Earth are you doing? Get away from my shop!

**George** (*lurching towards her*)    This is your shop, madam?

**Mrs Butcher**   Yes, mine and my husband's, but you're not going in: it's shut for the evening. There's a garage down the road if you're desperate.

**George**   I need to look inside.

**Mrs Butcher**   I'm sorry?

**George**   He's hiding in there, I need to look inside!

**Mrs Butcher**   There's no one hiding in there, I locked it up myself!

**George** (*banging on the shutters*)   Come out, you monster! Come out!

**Mr Butcher** *arrives, also in his dressing gown.*

**Mrs Butcher** (*to* **Mr Butcher**)   Did you call the police, Butcher?

**Mr Butcher**   I did.

**Mrs Butcher**   He's looking for someone inside, he keeps hammering on the shutters.

**Mr Butcher**   Look, I've called the police, pal, so just step away.

**George**   But he's in there! Let me in! Let me in!

*He starts kicking the shutters.*

Get out! Do you hear me?!

**Mrs Butcher**   Hey! Come on!

**George** *keeps kicking the shutters.* **Pike** *arrives.*

**Pike** (*arriving, to the* **Butchers**)   I've had a call about a drunk and disorderly: was that you?

**Mr Butcher**   It was.

**Mrs Butcher**   He just turned up and started kicking and punching our shutters. He thinks there's someone in there, Pike, we don't know what to do.

**Pike** (*moving towards* **George**)    Sir, I'm going to have to ask you to step back from the shop.

**George** (*still trying to get inside*)    No, I won't, not while he's in there.

**Pike**    Step back –

**George** (*still trying*)    I will not step back! I will not!

**Mrs Butcher**    He's not right in the head –

**Pike**    I won't ask you again, sir –

**George** *screams. He kicks and punches the shop, until it springs open. The inside stands revealed. It's empty. Silence.*

**Pike**    Sir! Come with me, please, you're under arrest.

**George**    Pike, no you can't. (*Removing his disguise.*) It's not – it's me, George.

**Mrs Butcher**    George! You're back!

**Pike**    Oh, I – Well, I'm not quite sure if I'm allowed to arrest Saint George.

**George** (*looking around*)    Did you see him? Which way did he go?

**Mrs Butcher**    If we'd have known it was you –

**George**    Did you see him? (*Turning on the* **Butchers**.) Unless he's one of you. Of course he is . . .

**Mr Butcher**    George –

**George** (*grabbing* **Mr Butcher**)    It's you, isn't it?! (*Assaulting him.*) Come on, monster show yourself! Show yourself!

**Mrs Butcher**    Get away from him! (*To* **Pike**.) Do something!

**Pike** (*grabbing and handcuffing* **George**)    Right, that's it. Saint George, you're under arrest.

**George** (*screaming at* **Mr Butcher**)    No, I know it's you! Show yourself!

**Pike**    You do not have to say anything –

**George**    Don't arrest me, arrest him!

**Pike**    But it may harm your defence –

**George**    Listen to me, Pike!

**Pike**    If you do not mention, when questioned –

**George**    I saw him, Pike! I saw him!

**Pike**    Something which you later rely on in court –

**George**    I swear to you, sir!

**Pike**    Anything you do say may be given in evidence –

**George**    Pike, you have to listen, he's –

**Pike**    You can rant as much as you want in the car. Come on.

*He leads* **George** *out. Silence.*

**Mrs Butcher**    Are you all right, Butcher?

**Mr Butcher**    I'll live.

**Mrs Butcher**    I didn't even know he was back. And then to see him like that!

**Mr Butcher**    I think something must be very wrong, love.

**Mr Butcher** *holds* **Mrs Butcher**.

**Mr Butcher**    Come on. Let's get you inside.

*They go.*


**Chapter XIII**
IN WHICH A CHOICE IS MADE

*The cells at the city police station, several hours later.* **George** *and* **Driver** *lie, asleep, in adjoining cells.* **Pike** *arrives, carrying a cup of water. He unlocks* **George**'s *cell and goes inside.*

**George** (*waking with a start*)    Where am I?

**Pike**    You know, I've had all sorts in here after a match, but never a dragon-slaying saint. You're at the police station, lad. (*Holding out the cup.*) I've brought you this.

**George**    No more strange drinks.

**Pike**    It's just water. Thought you might need it.

**George** *takes the water.*

**George**    Thank you, Pike.

**Pike** *goes.* **George** *thirstily drinks the water. He groans.*

**George**    Ugh, my head! What is this?!

**Driver**    It's called a hangover, Ian.

**George**    Driver?

**Driver**    It's all right, George. I know it's you.

**George**    Oh. Well. Listen, I may have said some things last night –

**Driver**    Don't worry about it. I've done my fair share of stupid stuff when I've been wasted: why d'you think I'm here? Although I never kicked the crap out of a minimart, but each to their own.

**George**    That was quite a bash you gave me. I deserved it, though.

**Driver**    You did.

**George**    Listen, Driver, I know you've never thought much of me –

**Driver**    That's not true, George. I may not be the best at showing it, but I've always respected you. That doesn't mean you didn't deserve a head-butt, but –

**George**    Thank you.

*Silence.*

**Driver**    I often think about that day, you know. The day when you first beat the Dragon. You weren't around to see it, cos that trumpet called you off by then, but we all stood together, we waved you goodbye and it was sunny and all the birds were singing. It was too late to work but too early to sleep, so we all just sat there, down by the river. The sun was out and the grass was dead soft, you know how it is by the side of the water. And we all just sat there. It was like a picnic. We ate and we talked and we lay on the bank and we drank as well, but none of us got wasted, mind, it was the kind of drunk where you're just hugging each other and laughing, you know, like a permanent four-pint level, and we were all just laughing so much and then it got dark and everyone went off to bed but not me, I just lay there in the soft grass and stared at the sky fading out, the little stars coming one by one, and I thought to myself: This. Is. Brilliant.

**George**   Do you ever see things, Driver?

**Driver**   Depends what I've been drinking.

**George**   I thought I saw someone before. Someone who ought to be dead.

**Driver**   I've heard that can happen.

**George**   Ugh.

**Driver**   You know what the best cure for a hangover is?

**George**   More alcohol?

**Driver**   Sleep. I'm gonna get my head down. I suggest you do the same.

**Driver** *lies down.* **George** *sits. The sound of footsteps returning.*

**George**   Oh, Pike, listen: I really ought to apologise –

*The* **Dragon** *appears, dressed as a policeman.*

**George**   You!

**Dragon**   And wouldn't it be lovely, George, if that was all I was: a figment of your tired and addled mind. But no. I'm here. And very much alive.

**George** *growls, reaches into his boot, pulls out his dagger and lashes out at the* **Dragon** *with it, through the bars.*

**Dragon**    Help! Help! He's got a weapon! Guard! Oh wait: that's me. What do you think of my new form?

**George**    Your new form?

**Dragon**    You see I'm a part of *them* now: I'm the shrug of their shoulders, the nothing-to-be-done, the shouting, the pointing, the misdirected anger, the despair. D'you remember when I told you that I wanted to crush all that's good in them? Until they become me? Well, as you can see, I'm not doing badly at all. I'm growing, inside them, George, with every passing minute. And soon they will be fully mine.

**George**    They'll never surrender to you, Dragon.

**Dragon**    Perhaps not. But, unlike you, I don't need some grand decisive victory. I'm winning little by little, day by dull and steady day. In times gone by if someone dropped a bushel of apples at the market they'd all rush running to their aid. If somebody was ill, they'd all bring broth. But watch them now: even if someone's lying bleeding in the street, these days the greater part of them will cross to the other side. And it won't be long before they trample them.

**George**    I'll vanquish you again, I always do.

**Dragon**    Not this time. I live inside every single one of them now. Man, woman and child. So what are you going to do, slice me out of them with a dagger? (**George** *is silent.*)Then it's time to face the truth, Saint George: you've lost.

*He goes.*

**George**    Wait! Wait! Come back here! Wait – (*He clutches his head.*) Ow, too loud.

**Pike** *arrives.*

**Pike**    Calm it down, George.

**George**    Oh, Pike, I'm sorry, I –

**Pike**   You've got a visitor.

**George**   Elsa?!

**Charles** *arrives.*

**Charles**   Not quite.

**Pike** (*going*)   I'll leave you to it.

**Charles**   A drunken rampage after the football, followed by a night in the cells: I know you wanted to integrate back into the community, George, but this is taking it a bit far, don't you think?

**George**   I know, Charles, but –

**Charles**   You've done a great deal of damage to the Butchers' shop, it's a wonder they're not pressing charges –

**George**   And I'm sorry, I am –

**Charles**   Well I've brought you a toothbrush and a nice clean shirt –

**George**   No, Charles, please, just listen to me for a moment –

**Charles**   The shirt's one of mine so I'm not sure it'll fit you, but –

**George**   The Dragon's back, Charles! The Dragon's back, and he's in all of you now! He's in all of you!

*Silence.*

**Charles**   We know, George.

*Silence.*

**George**   You know?

**Charles**   Of course we do. We know very well that he's here. I can feel him right now, and it's horrible.

**George**   Then why aren't you fighting?

**Charles**   We're trying! Why d'you think Elsa gets up every day and goes to a job that she hates? Why do I keep plugging away with that microwave even though I've nearly burned the house down four times? Why do we drink, and fight, and end up in here? Because we're trying, in any way that we can, to pull ourselves out of the despair that he's pushing us into! To quieten down his voice in our heads. We're doing all we can, George.

**George**   Well, you don't need to worry any more, Charles, because I'm back and I'm going to save you!

**Charles**   How?

**George**   I, I don't know yet, but –

**Charles** (*suddenly darker, more serious*)   We can't be saved, George. It just can't be done. So pull yourself together. Brush your teeth. Then come home. You owe my daughter an apology.

**George**   Charles –

**Charles** (*back to breezy tones*)   I got some nice bacon from the shop, I can cook us some breakfast. It's supposed to be bright out this morning, so we can all sit outside, have a little picnic, if you like. I'll see you soon.

*He goes. Silence.* **George** *stands and thinks.*

**George** (*to himself*)   A picnic . . . (*Calling out.*) Pike! Pike!

**Pike** *returns.*

**Pike**   Not long till sun-up, lad. Then I'll let you out.

**George**   Pike, will you do something for me?

**Pike**   Now, George –

**George**   Please, Pike, for me. For me.

**Pike**   What is it?

**George**   Have Crier call everyone together.

**Pike**   What?

**George**   Gather them all outside, in the square.

**Pike**   George –

**George**   Please, Pike. You've put your faith in me in the past, and it's always been rewarded, hasn't it? So please trust me this one last time.

*Silence.*

**Pike**   Okay.

*He goes.*

**George** (*calling after him*)   You won't regret it, Pike! I'll finish this, once and for all!


## Chapter the Last
IN WHICH SAINT GEORGE ISSUES HIS FINAL CHALLENGE

*The street outside the city police station, in the first grey light of the morning. It's cold, and slightly damp. The city folk, bleary-eyed and anxious, begin to gather, household by household.* **Elsa** *and* **Charles** *are not present.*

**Miller**   I hope this won't take long: he (**Young Miller**) needs to get to work.

**Healer**   What's all this about, Crier?

**Crier**   Your guess is as good as mine. He wants to talk to us, is all I know.

**Mrs Butcher**   You all ought to have seen him last night, the way he attacked our shop, it was frightening. He had at Mr Butcher's shoulder, too. He's not in his right mind.

**Brewer**   You should've seen the state of my pub: broken glass everywhere, chairs smashed to pieces, blood on the floor –

**Smith** (*to the* **Boy**)   What were you thinking, bringing him to a pub on a match day?

**Boy**   I was just trying to cheer him up.

**Crier**   Oh leave him, Smith, he wasn't to know. And we all got a bit lairy last night, didn't we?

**Son**   Too right.

**Alice**   Regretting it now, though.

**Driver** and **Pike** *emerge from the police station, followed by* **George**. **George** *looks wrecked and haggard, slightly wild.*

**Boy**   George!

**Smith**   How are you feeling, George?

**Healer**   We really didn't know it was you last night, George.

**George**   Don't worry, Healer, it's – (*He breathes.*) Thank you for coming out here so early, my friends. How am I feeling, Smith? Awful. I need to apologise. For your pub, Brewer. Your shop, Mrs Butcher. (*To* **Mr Butcher**.) Your shoulder. I'm so sorry, all of you. Something terrible happened to me last night. Something I've never – I wasn't myself, is what I mean. And I thought it was the football, or us losing, or the argument, or the alcohol. But it wasn't. I mean, all of those things did happen, but it wasn't any of them, it was *him*. It was the Dragon. He got in here – (*Pointing to his head.*) just like he's got to every one of you. He's crawled inside your heads, inside your hearts. He's drained your hope and your strength, and he's chipped away at your spirit. And it won't be long until he's won, until all the good in you is gone, until he's peopled this island with dragons, and we can't let that happen.

**Crier**   George, what are you –

**George**   Please, Crier, hear me out. We have to get rid of him once and for all.

**Son**   We've tried!

**George**   I know, I know you have, but I'm not saying – Look, he's one step ahead of you: he always has been.

**Healer's Daughter**   So what do we –

**George**   We have to do something we've never done before.

**Mrs Butcher**   Like what?

**George**   I should never have left, you see. The first time I vanquished the Dragon, with all of you standing right here and willing me on, I left straight afterwards. But Driver, you told me just now of the rest of that day, of you all sitting, talking, laughing in the grass. You were free that day, and I never got to see it because I was gone. But don't you want it back again?

**Brewer**   What do you mean 'want it back'?

**George**   That's how we beat him. We go back. To what we were before. To what we were that day. Before he got – (*Pointing to his head.*) in here, to when everything was ours.

**Healer**   But, George –

**George**   And that's how we win. You said it yourselves and I was too stupid, too frightened to listen: he's in all of this. And I just said 'make more', 'our happiness is yet to come', I said: but we had our happiness, that day. And the only way to get rid of him for good is to go back there.

**Pike**   But how?

**George**   Tear it all down, all of it, the buildings, the bridges, the lights, tear all of it down, until this whole island is meadow once more, until everything he's feeding off is gone. Until we belong to ourselves again. That's how we beat him. That's how we win.

*Silence.*

What do you say?

*The city folk look at each other.*

Don't you miss it? Knowing what you're for? Waking up with the sun? (*To* **Driver**.) Falling asleep with the stars coming out –

**Driver**   It was a good day, George. But that's all it was: one day.

**George**   With not a dragon in sight.

**Driver**   Look, we get it, George, but –

**George**  Don't you want to defeat him? Don't you want to be happy again?

**Crier**  We're happy now, George. Sometimes. Nights in the pub when we're all there together I've been crying with laughter. We have good days and bad.

**George**  But the Dragon –

**Crier**  He's there, of course he's there. But he hasn't won.

**Pike**  He hasn't got us, George.

**George**  It's only a matter of time –

**Smith**  With all due respect, George, and respect is due, absolutely, but you were the one who told us to keep going. You stood right here and you told us to carry on, and now you're telling us to go back?

**Son**  He's right, George. And all the glory and all the compromise and the suffering, it's all the same thing, you know.

**George**  No, I know, but I was wrong, I didn't realise we'd be opening the door –

**Mr Butcher**  George.

**George**  And letting the Dragon –

**Mr Butcher**  George.

**George**  But it's not too late, it's –

**Mr Butcher**  George, will you just listen for a minute?! Now I know that he's back, and I understand what you're asking us to do, but this is our home. And we've spent our lives making it. So I don't think you're allowed to just turn up here and tell us to tear it down.

**George**  Allowed? It's my home too, I was born here too; and might I remind you it's my cross that flies over this isle?

**Brewer**  Now, George –

**George**  I have suffered and fought and bled in your name –

**Miller**   But, George –

**George**   I have risked my life again and again for the good of this place –

**Driver**   But –

**George**   I am Saint George the Dragon-slayer, and you must join me in this fight!

*He is shouting quite loudly.* **Elsa** *and* **Charles** *arrive.*

**Elsa**   What's going on, George?

**Charles**   Where were you? We were waiting –

**George**   I know how to beat him, Charles. It's so simple but they just won't –

**Elsa**   What are you talking about?

**George**   He's going to win unless we do something, he said it himself: he's inches away from victory.

**Mrs Butcher**   But we can't –

**George**   We've got to shut him out, tear it all down, starve him, go back to the day I first killed him and wall ourselves off so he can never get to us again.

**Elsa**   Please, George –

**George**   Help me convince them, Elsa. It will be as if I never left in the first place.

**Elsa**   But you did leave, George. You left and we stayed here. And we survived. We're here now, George. We can't go back.

**George**   Elsa –

**Elsa**   I've lived in a village. I've worked in a field. I've put my hands into the earth. I've drawn water from a well. I've slept on a bed made of straw. I've lived in a town. A whistle called me to work. It was hot, it was dark, my fingers bled, the frames shook all around me, the sky, our sky, outside, was full of smoke. I've lived in a city, where it's loud. Where the lights are so bright they make me wince and my work follows me home in the evening. We've lived lifetimes, George. Each one of us here. We've come too far to go back now.

**George**    There's still time, Elsa –

**Elsa**    No, George.

**George**    Please, listen –

**Charles**    We are listening, George. But the world isn't a ride you can stop whenever you fancy. We have a duty to the time we're living in. Like it or not. However hard it may be, Elsa is right.

**George**    I don't understand.

**Elsa**    Of course you don't, George. And that's why I love you. You're perfect, clean lines. Like a stained-glass window. A picture in a story book. But we're not that simple any more. We're staying here.

**George** (*imploring*)    No, no, that's him talking now. That's the Dragon. I can hear him in you, he's screaming with laughter. That's why you won't listen, isn't it?

**Elsa**    George, stop it. Now. Come home. Please.

**George**    You have to let me help you, Elsa: you have to let me save you.

**Elsa**    But we don't need saving any more.

**Henry** (*moving to join* **Elsa**)    She's right.

**George**    Oh, you would say that, wouldn't you?

**Henry**    No, all I mean is –

**George**    The Dragon's faithful little servant.

**Elsa**    George, he's not –

**George**    Stay out of this, Elsa.

**Henry**    Look, just leave her alone.

**George**  Oh, I see what this is: he's in love with you! (*Laughs.*) He's in love with you, Elsa, that's what this is –

**Elsa**  George –

**George**  Am I wrong, Henry? Tell me I'm wrong.

**Elsa**  Henry, it's –

**Henry**  No, it's fine. He's right.

**George**  You see!

**Elsa**  What?

**Henry**  I love you, Elsa, I –

**Elsa**  Since when?

**Henry**  I don't remember. Since that night in the prison? Or maybe since we were small, I'm not sure. But I do.

**George** (*to everyone*)  See?

**Henry**  But that's not why I – That's not what this is about, George. I know you want to fight him, but the Dragon's in us now, so this is our battle, not yours.

**George**  And there he is: the Dragon speaks! You've been his man since the very beginning.

**Henry**  No, George –

**George**  I can see him sitting there inside you, smirking out from behind your eyes –

**Elsa**  George –

**George**  Well, I'll cut him out of you if that's what it takes!

*He draws his dagger.*

Dragon, I challenge you!

**Pike** (*stepping forward*)  Put the knife down, lad.

**George**  No!

**Pike** *moves to apprehend* **George** *but* **George** *slices him across the arm.* **Pike** *falls. Some of the city folk step back, others move to protect* **Henry**.

**Elsa**    George, please –

**Driver**    George –

**George**    You'd choose the Dragon's servant over your champion, over your freedom?!

**Boy**    George –

**Brewer**    George –

*Pike's* **Son** *tries to bundle* **Henry** *away.* **George** *lunges at him, but* **Crier** *and* **Smith** *push* **George** *back.*

**George**    It's too late, then: he's taken you all!

**Young Miller** *runs at* **George** *and* **George** *stabs him. Screams.*

**Charles**    George –

**Elsa**    George –

*For a brief moment the* **Dragon** *seems to appear in the crowd.*

**George**    He's there! He's there!

*The city folk form a circle around* **George**.

I'll cut him out of you!

*He lashes out whenever they get close.*

Out of each and every one of you!

**Crier**, **Driver** *and* **Smith** *charge at* **George** *from behind and wrestle the dagger out of his hand.* **Crier** *kicks it away.* **George** *throws them off him, kicking* **Healer's Daughter** *in the process.*

**George**    Get off –

*He charges at* **Henry**, *knocks him over and begins to strangle him. Some people try to pull* **George** *off* **Henry**, *but his hands remain clamped around his throat. The* **Boy** *sees the dagger on the floor, near to* **Elsa**.

**Boy** (*pointing at the dagger*)   Elsa! Quick! Do something!

**Elsa** *grabs the dagger and plunges it into* **George**'s *back. He dies.*

*A very long silence. The city folk comfort each other, and tend to the wounded. Some are crying, some are too shocked to speak.* **Charles** *holds* **Elsa**.

**Charles**   It's okay, love, it's okay . . .

*More silence. Then, very slowly, the city folk start to look at one another, and after a while, whenever the air feels ready,* **Brewer** *quietly asks the question:*

**Brewer**   What now?

*The* **Boy** *slowly stands and goes to the centre. Then each of the city folk, grouped by household, helping each other to stand, if necessary, go and line up next to him.* **Elsa** *and* **Charles** *are the last. And they stand there, all in a line: bruised, bloody, almost broken, with the weight of whole centuries bearing down on their backs. But still together, somehow. Somehow, still alive.*

**Boy**   Close your eyes.

*They do. And the soft morning sunshine, the kind you only get on this little island of ours, breaks through the clouds up above, comes down, and gently warms their faces for a while.*

For a complete listing of Bloomsbury
Methuen Drama titles, visit:
**www.bloomsbury.com/drama**

Follow us on Twitter and keep up to date
with our news and publications
**@MethuenDrama**